HOPE FOR MAN IN A HOPELESS WORLD

BY
BASILEA SCHLINK

Translated by M. D. Rogers
and Larry Christenson

DIMENSION BOOKS
Bethany Fellowship, Inc.
Minneapolis, Minnesota

DIMENSION BOOKS
are published by
Bethany Fellowship, Inc.
6820 Auto Club Road
Minneapolis, Minnesota 55438

Scripture quotations are from the Revised Standard
Version, copyright 1946 and 1952 by the Division
of Christian Education of the National Council
of Churches of Christ, and are used by permission.
Library of Congress Catalog Card Number 67-11614

Originally published under the title:
AND NONE WOULD BELIEVE IT
© 1967 by Zondervan Publishing House
All rights reserved
MANUFACTURED IN THE U.S.A.

CONTENTS

I. MORAL LANDSLIDE!
How Could Things Reach This Stage?........11

The Present Situation 11

*Causes in the Realm of the History of
   Human Intellect During the Past
   Two Centuries* 33

Causes in the Realm of Theology 46

II. IS THERE STILL HOPE? 62

The Reality of the Other Kingdom 62

*Laws of the Kingdom — an Unchanging
   Offer of Divine Love* 72

*God's Commandments — Still Binding
   Today? Relevant or Outmoded?* 81

*Resistance to God's Commandments —
   Why?* 86

*Workers Together With God —
   Today's Greatest Need* 95

III. REALLY THE END OF TIME?
Nobody Believes It 103

I.

MORAL LANDSLIDE —
HOW COULD THINGS REACH THIS STAGE?

The Present Situation

AT A SMALL THEATER in the vicinity of the Vatican in Rome, hundreds of enthusiastic young people attended a performance of the play *Christ 1963* by Camillo Beni. The crucifixion of Christ is portrayed as a bacchanalian orgy. Christ smells of alcohol. Mary Magdalene, who bends over him, is a prostitute. The most holy becomes "food for swine." Sometimes the light goes out and the theater becomes a house of carnal desire. One article reported on it in the following way: "The devil no longer deems it necessary to disguise himself. The devil makes his entrance right into the Eternal City."[1] The theater was finally closed. Just an oddity, perhaps? One of those embarrassing things that happen from time to time?

Not so. This play was closed due to its base derision of something holy. But its theme of naked sexuality and brutality is powerfully alive in movies and on the stage today. In New York the play *The Toilet* was sold out during virtually the entire summer of 1965, normally a slack theater season. The stage setting was a toilet in a public school. Several Negroes and two white students come in during the breaks between classes. In one scene, one of the white boys is beaten almost to death. Homosexuality is one of the dominant themes. The

---

[1] *Revue*, February, 1964

dialogue is way-out slang and jazz talk, with a heavy accent on brutality.[2]

Recently the London Theatrical Academy (LAMDA) has been rising in fame. It has been dubbed "The Theater of Cruelty." On its stage the basest passions and crass carnality parade boldly in the limelight. "A surrealistic revue," says one critic, "intended to destroy the sense of shame associated with such abnormal and shameless words and gestures."[3]

Nor is this just an odd or occasional occurrence. European theaters from London to Vienna portray torture scenes with utmost realism: The blood-lust cries of the torturers, the screams of pain from the tortured, with stereophonic sound effects of bones breaking; abortions portrayed on the open stage; until one finally raises the question: Why not portray the sex act itself out on the stage?[4]

The theater of today is more and more taking on the role of portraying the collapse of all order and restraint, whether it be in this form or in the grotesque.

And what of the movies?

In 1964 Sweden produced Ingmar Bergman's film *The Silence*. It received wide publicity, both in the secular press and in Christian publications. It has been seen by great throngs of people, and is now making its rounds of the world. It shows the tortured lives of two sisters who live together, sunk in the depths of a soulless sexuality. Bergman uses this situation of total human confusion to interpret "being in hell"; the godless world, the lost condition of man who seems doomed to fall into the hands of a senseless fate. No life worth living remains for man. God is silent and man is without hope. The only thing left open to him is naked sexuality.

---

[2] *Die Welt*, February 26, 1965
[3] Roland Hill, "Grausames Theater in London," *Frankfurter Allgemeine Zeitung (FAZ)*, February 13, 1964
[4] *FAZ*, November 29, 1965

There is no way out of this confused wilderness and senselessness — so say the newspapers — other than a plunge into the immoral life of animal desire such as the close-ups of this film portray. The last taboos are swept away. That which was previously known only in off-color "stag parties" and hard core pornography has now become the theme of successful and famous films, and stage productions as well.

And such films as *The Silence* are classed by film censoring authorities as "especially worthwhile." Even Catholic and Protestant members of the censoring board raised no objection. They contended that here a shocking presentation serves to warn us where a life of nihilism, without God, finally leads. But the means which the film employs are dangerous. Anyone who thinks that he needs to display misused sexuality before our eyes, in order to warn us of the godlessness and nihilism of our time, must realize at what cost this is done. He becomes guilty of perverting the actors, including a child, who portray these scenes. He becomes guilty of misleading the millions of young people who watch such scenes, and then are stimulated to go out and commit the same things. What used to be dealt with in the courtroom, behind closed doors, in now displayed publicly.

Promoters of such films contend that if depravity is shown with "relentless candor," virtue will come to the fore in a healthy counterreaction. But no one is going to be cured of perversity by having a good look at it. On the contrary, that which I look at influences me. Poison which I drink will make me sick. Poison, and above all the poison of sin, at all costs must be shunned and fought against. Otherwise it will bring about the downfall of a man, a people, indeed of humanity itself. The disgust one experiences at seeing such depravity does not evoke "a healthy counterreaction": It merely makes life senseless. Even worse, as *Christ und Welt* observed, "you invite Death to be your guest."[5] That is the actual end result.

Significantly Sweden, the source of this and similar films, is a country with one of the highest suicide rates — which shows the result of such an attitude. People are driven along the road of sin, disgust with life, and death. And a third of the customers for these kinds of films are young people.

But who takes it seriously? Research at the University of Wisconsin indicates some frightening correlations: The danger of brutal movies and TV programs cannot be passed off; powerful momentary stimulation to feelings of hate and rage begets a readiness toward aggressive behavior, even in perfectly normal people; such a feeling of aggression can be easily triggered to spend itself in overt acts.[6] Yet the army of spokesmen for such films continues to grow. They do not realize how they have fallen prey to a highly lucrative business operation, which exploits shameless sexual indiscretion and unrestrained immorality at great profit. And the public, so a newspaper reports, having once gotten the "sex scent," develops a craving for increasingly stronger doses of "sex nourishment." Those who rose to stardom in Hollywood films during 1965 did so in varying stages of undress — not only women, but men, too. Mr. Shurlock, vice-president of the film industry association, said, "Our morals have changed as much as our business. It's not surprising that our films take notice of this."[7]

"A comparison of the titles, contents, and advertisements of films from ten years ago shows clearly a constantly increased sexual pressure upon the individual. Today the movies no longer present great themes. Love has degenerated to sexuality, to mere naked desire. One can only view these

---
[5] Hans Schomerus, "Das Gastmahl des Lasters," *Christ und Welt,* April 3, 1964
[6] *Jugendschutz-Materialdienst,* January, 1965
[7] *Neue Illustrierte,* August 29, 1965

films today with shame. Everything in them is calculated to stimulate passion. Three themes attract: sensation, sex, and sentimentality, and in the long run it is making money that counts."[8]

And now movies are beginning to get competition from television, with its fare of "adult programs" — knowing, of course, that television will also be feeding this fare to children with mealtime regularity. "This is a certain step towards the utter destruction of moral standards," writes an American newspaper man. Because of this competition, the movies have to go even deeper into the sex-business. And it is crowned with success: sex attracts the masses. It is no wonder that Lesslie Newbigin, Bishop of the Church of South India, writes about the spreading of Western literature and the influence of the film in his book *One World — One Faith*: "In India the ubiquitous cinema has been the means of introducing almost all strata of the population, in the most vivid possible way, to conceptions of ethics so much lower than their own as to make nonsense of any claim by the West to moral leadership. It would not be too gross an exaggeration to say that for many in the East, the West stands for three things: war, sex, and technics." In all of this we can see a part of the collapse of the West taking place before our very eyes, but who wishes to believe it?

The decay of moral standards and the rotting away of moral fiber has ravaged the world of literature as well. Even a few years ago, such books would have been found only in the murky world of trash and pornography. Today they are common even in educated circles. In the mixing of modern ideas, pornography often comes out as the theme in a piece of modern literature. The level of moral standards has sunk so low that a first edition of the book *Memoirs of a Woman of Pleasure — Fanny Hill* was entirely sold out before it was

---

[8]*Sueddeutsche Zeitung*, March 14, 1964

off the press. It was bound in silk, printed on the finest quality paper, and sold for $15 — a "collector's item." A second and third edition had to be printed before the first was even completed.

This kind of poison is spreading throughout the entire world in epidemic proportions. The general situation of the world abets it. Never before could one say that the world could be regarded as a unit. But today modern communications have fashioned a kind of world-wide unity. Nations and peoples know everything that happens in other parts of the world the same day it happens. In the decisive issues, all men have a common life and common fate. This became clear at the time of the Cuban crisis. Our horizon is no longer European or American or Asian, but world-wide, embracing all humanity. What significance does this have for the mood of immorality and corruption in our modern age? The frightening fact is this: for the first time, decadence and lawlessness hold sway over a majority of the nations of earth. Through the continuous spread of literature, films, and television, these influences have circled the globe. Such was never before the case. Certainly immorality and crime have always existed. But it was always of a local nature, occurring first in one country, then in another. On the whole, however, God's commandments were widely recognized as moral standards, and were a dam against unrestrained immorality.

Today we find that this dam has collapsed in most places. More and more, all nations are coming to share a common political fate. Thus they are becoming more and more subject to the same spirit, the spirit of lawlessness. This is a sign that the "latter days" are upon us.

The degree to which this spirit grips each country is brought out in reports coming from various countries. For example, in the United States over the last four years, the number of registered criminal offenses has increased four times as quickly as the population. The number of bank robberies has almost tripled in six years. Larceny has increased by 15% since 1958.[9] The FBI's 1965 Statistical Report records a shocking increase in sexual offenses. In a single year rape cases increased by 21%.[10] America, which has lived for 300 years under the impress of the Puritan ethic, openly tabbed 1963 as "The Year of Lust."[11] Newspapers in the United States speak of a "moral landslide." For the first time publications are appearing in which lust is not merely tolerated, but exalted. Helen Gurley Brown, the "most read authoress," writes frankly on the subject of sexuality.[12]

In France, Johnny Halliday has similar success with his records, which have the same theme: desire must be fulfilled. They are sold by the million. With the help of a radio station, Halliday gathered together 150,000 young people on a June evening in 1963. Youngsters between the ages of 12 and 20 thronged la Place de la Nation in Paris. They bawled and whistled in a mad frenzy, as if under the influence of mass-psychosis.[13]

In Austria a "Sex Party" has entered the political arena. Its platform calls for the abolishment of all laws against abortion and homosexuality. In Austria alone, 600,000 women have undergone abortion, and about 750,000 persons are either homosexual or bisexual.[14]

In Germany, also, there are factions opposing the laws against homosexuality. Doctors even speak of the "ethical

---

[9] *U. S. News and World Report,* August 26, 1963
[10] *Christ und Welt,* August 27, 1965
[11] *Newsweek* — quoted in *Die Zeit,* December 27, 1963
[12] *Stern* — quoted in a prospectus Franz Decker Verlag, Schmiden bei Stuttgart.
[13] *Die Zeit,* August 16, 1963
[14] *Jodioth Chadaschoth,* March 19, 1964

value of a homosexual partnership."[15] Lawyers have determined that "homosexuality is at least as common as adultery and prostitution," and demand a readjustment of the law to reflect the true social conditions.[16] The burgeoning prostitution business in West Germany cities has given rise in Hamburg to "Sky Scrapers of Delight" for six hundred "ladies."[17] Investigations have revealed that every fifth twenty-year-old living in this city has had recourse to a prostitute.[18]

From England, renowned for its puritan morals in earlier times, comes the alarming report of an Inquiry Commission: Between 1950 and 1961 the number of illegitimate babies born to girls in the age group of 11 to 16 increased threefold.[19] In February, 1963, the highly respected Sunday newspaper *The Observer* published the following comment of the Glasgow Student's Union: "The day will soon come when pre-marital intercourse will be no more risky and no more frowned upon than pre-marital kissing (very sinful in Victorian days) is at present time."[20]

In view of Sweden's film production, it is not surprising that a brisk debate is going on in the nation's newspapers on the subject of sexual excesses among juveniles. In the schools, 14 to 17-year-old girls receive instruction on methods of contraception. In this controversy, the younger doctors say, "It is reactionary, dangerous, and stupid to regard lifelong marriage as the only condition for intercourse between the sexes. Such a viewpoint is an offense to those who cannot marry. The sexual sphere of life is a private, not a public matter."[21]

---

[15] *Die Zeit*, April 3, 1964
[16] *Die Zeit*, April 10, 1964
[17] *Die Zeit*, February 22, 1963
[18] Urich Beer, *Geheime Miterzieher der Jugend,* Verlag Walter Rawh, 1960, p. 63.
[19] *FAZ*, March 8, 1964
[20] *Die Zeit*, February 15, 1964
[21] *Darmstaedter Echo*, March 1964

Up until a few years ago, Japan was well known for having virtually no juvenile crime. Yet today she is being plagued with organized crime and increasing juvenile delinquency. In recent months, Japanese authorities have found themselves more and more occupied with increasing hold-ups, theft, abduction, and knife fights. Three sixteen-year-old Tokyo schoolboys pulled seven robberies within the space of three and a half hours. The reason? "For fun." The unfavorable influence of television and detective stories and the dissolution of family structure are some of the causes behind this. In addition to juvenile crime, organized gangsterism is on the rise in Japan. In 1963 the police ascertained that there were more than 5000 gangster organizations in Japan, with more than 180,000 members.[22]

Up until now the pioneer state of Israel has recorded but few cases of criminal activity and moral breakdown. Yet even there the dam is now breaking. The newspaper *Jedioth Chadaschoth* reported on February 14, 1964 that "robbery of women has become the order of the day, mostly by youthful aggressors . . . the streets of Jerusalem are becoming increasingly unsafe."

The avalanche is now poised and ready to plunge down upon the under-developed nations. The situation is already ripe. Western culture and technology are not in themselves a negative factor. But without any root of ethical values, and without historical growth they have invaded the nations of Asia and Africa. This invasion has rocked previous foundations. The customs and systems which the under-developed nations inherited from their forefathers have been swept away to a great extent, together with their pagan beliefs which did provide some sort of barrier. Ten years ago no one would have believed that today young Chinese would open the graves of their ancestors and scatter the ashes on the fields. A

---

[22]*FAZ*, April 22, 1964

religious tradition which had been reverenced by the nation for thousands of years has been reduced to a ridiculous practice by the vaunting of "rational principles."

We live in an age of irreverence, the starting-point for immorality. With the fall of their gods and idols, these nations are presented with even more fearful idols: nicotine, narcotics and alcohol; bad movies, pornography — indeed the whole degeneracy of the white peoples. These nations are even less protected against such forces than the Occident. Missionaries from South Africa report that in the so-called "locations," the swamp of iniquity is widening. In a location of 200,000 inhabitants, 50,000 are given over to practicing prostitution, which means that virtually every young girl is involved.[23]

Mankind is gripped by a veritable intoxication of sexual desire and brutality, and along with this has come a primitive mania for narcotics. This evil is sweeping into the Western world like a flood. Today, more than ever before, people are seeking intoxication in the form of narcotics such as hashish, opium, and marijuana cigarettes.

In the fall of 1965, the World Health Organization in Geneva determined that "the spread of narcotic addiction among juveniles has reached epidemic proportions." They called for drastic control measures. Also in need of stricter controls, according to the same report, are the hundreds of far-from-harmless pep pills and tranquilizers.[24]

In 1963 narcotic addicts in the United States numbered 60,000 — a fourth of them under 20 years of age. By 1965 the figure had climbed to 100,000. Through physical fitness exams for military service, it has come to light that in some schools up to 90% of the students smoke marijuana. The "dream cigarette," at $1.25 each, seemingly harmless,

---
[23]*Nachrichten der Dorothea - Mission, S*eptember 1963
[24]*FAZ*, November 1, 1965

goes from hand to hand as an everyday affair. And so one begins to see in the headlines, "Narcotic-Cigarettes Hit the School Yard."[25]

A humanity which has lost the ground under its feet and which thus seeks escape in drugs, also increasingly seeks after "thrills" and "shocks." In West Germany, for instance, a television series portrayed one murder after another. During the time of broadcast the streets were empty and public events languished for customers. Millions sat in front of their televison sets watching the grisly sensation as if under a spell.

The report of a committee of the United States Senate pointed out the frequency of murders on the American television screen: every week about one hundred and fifty victims are publicly shot, beaten to death, strangled, knifed, thrown out of a window or from a cliff-edge, and sometimes tortured to death in the most fiendish fashion. All this takes place before the eyes of millions of American men, women and children.[26]

A survey of eight and nine-year-old school children turned up the fact that they were all keen viewers of crime films on television. They particularly liked it when a murder, a shooting, or at least a fight took place before their eyes. "I always like it when they kill somebody. My head gets all hot," one child wrote.[27]

What are some of the consequences of this morbid interest in brutality? "During and after the period when a crime-serial 'The Scarf' ran, statisticians recorded six scarf-murders."[28]

Beset by emptiness and boredom, mankind seeks intoxication, thrills, and shock-effects . . . often hungers after the

---
[25]*Evangelisches Darmstadt,* June 6, 1965
[26]*Fuer jedermann!* Kitchener, Ontario, Number 68, January 1960
[27]*Stuttgarter Zeitung,* April 14, 1964
[28]*Die Zeit,* December 13, 1964

basest animal sensations. We not only have a "Theater of Cruelty": The world of professional sports lays an increasing accent on raw brutality.

When world heavyweight boxing champion Cassius Clay says that he will "punish" his opponent, thousands of customers — and millions of television viewers — turn out to see him do just that.

Within the highly skilled maneuvers of professional football is an element of brutality which frightens even the participants. An orthopedic surgeon who serves as staff physician to one of the professional football teams says, "These pro football players are a strange breed. They're physical freaks — their size and strength and prowess is way beyond the average. But down underneath they're actually scared. They know that out there on the field they're going to meet up with another team of gladiators that is just as big and just as strong as they are — and anything could happen." One sportswriter candidly refers to the game as "legalized manslaughter."

The fantastic rise in the popularity of professional football in recent years is accurately mirrored in the six-figure "bonus" commanded by a good college star when he signs a contract.

History shows that the mania for brutal sensation is a typical sign of nations facing their downfall. But no one notices it, no one believes it. Even in the fellowship of true Christian believers, one does not see the truth of it. Yet the enemy of God raises his head more defiantly then ever, betraying the lateness of the hour in which we live. For when the world of the living God (for most people) falls away, the world of the enemy rises up — Satan, with his demons, superstitions, and soothsaying.

This ought to wake us up. It points up the Powers that are at work behind the breakdown of morals, the brutality, and the vice of our day. In an introduction to Paul Bauer's *Horoscope and Talisman*, Kurt Hutten writes, "The flood of superstition has risen sharply. It forms a huge 'confession,' which is subdivided into numerous denominations. Rank superstition has crystallized in so many concrete forms and expressions that one can no longer overlook it."[29]

In West Germany about twenty million people read their horoscopes regularly. Fifteen million admit to believing in astrology. Eight million direct their lives according to it. And this in a country renowned for its scientific and rational achievements.[30] Indeed, our entire age proudly declares that it is the age of the greatest discoveries in science, the age of space research — the age which has outgrown the traditional Christian faith. Yet "rank superstition" is markedly on the rise.

Man contends today that the Christian faith can no longer speak a sure word in regard to morals and ethics. Many voices rise in agreement — both inside and outside the Church. With respect to birth control, for instance, social anthropologists have put forward the following radical thesis: "At a time in which the continued existence of mankind is at stake, Christian-Occidental ethics have become immoral. They make continued reference to the dubious judgments of a man from Nazareth who lived two thousand years ago and who understood nothing of the modern world. The refrain runs: 'ethics must be changed.'[31] Here we see the principles of the New Testament facing an "ethic of expediency," with its almost compulsive bent to adapt itself to the spirit of the times.

On November 11, 1964, the German newspaper *Die Zeit* wrote that the woman of today shys away from the responsibilities of marriage and motherhood because she is reluctant to take upon herself the sacrifice which real marriage and motherhood involves. A significant number of doctors go

---

[29]Einleitung zu Paul Bauer, *Horoskop und Talisman*, Quellverlag 1963
[30]Ulrich Beer, op. cit., page 60
[31]*Die Zeit*, February 14, 1964

along with this attitude and call for general distribution of the so-called "anti-baby-pills." The college doctor at the University of Sheffield began to dispense these pills on demand.[32] It has always been considered the calling and proper concern of a doctor to help keep the rhythm of life healthy and normal. But in protecting from the danger of pregnancy, the anti-baby-pills must disturb the physical and psychological rhythm of a woman's life. It is a violent intrusion into God's creative order.

The very name "anti-baby-pill" is a sign of disintegration. A Munich neurologist has said, "The word 'anti-baby-pill' itself speaks volumes. A pill which prevents maw-worms from coming into existence could be termed an anti-maw-worm-pill. Analogous to this, an anti-baby-pill is one which prevents babies from coming into existence. The casual use of this term betrays the questionable ethical orientation of the person who invented the term, and of those who agree with and use it."

"The cost of anti-baby-pills should be covered by medical insurance," says the Public Health Director of a large city. At the same time, a move is afoot to do away with police authority to prevent wide-open advertising of contraceptives.[33]

It goes without saying that uninhibited sexual expression, both in public and private, leads to the disintegration of a people and a culture. We stand on the brink of our own destruction.

A life of animal instincts, desire for sensation, superstition, and decadence in every field — such is the picture of humanity in our time. Wherever one looks, ethical foundations have crumbled. Mankind seems about to be swallowed up in an unbelievable quagmire of rottenness. God once said of all mankind living upon the earth, "The wickedness of man

---

[32]*Die Welt*, February 18, 1965
[33]*Constanze*, Fruehjahr 1964

is great in the earth" (Genesis 6:5). The judgment is frighteningly true today! And God said further, "I will blot out man whom I have created from the face of the ground" (Genesis 6:7). No one believed it then. But the Great Flood came.

And today, who believes that a quagmire of sin threatens to devour mankind? Who believes that sin increases in intensity year after year? Month by month we hear of the frightening spread of perversity and shamelessness. It hardly seems possible that these things could be "surpassed," and yet they are. But who really believes it?

There was One who prophesied it — Jesus. Of the latter days He said, "As were the days of Noah, so will be the coming of the Son of man . . ." (Matthew 24:37). In the latter days the condition of mankind will closely approximate the condition of mankind prior to the Flood. And Jesus prophesied further concerning these latter days: As in the days of the Great Flood, once again men will be destroyed — unless . . . yes, unless they repent and turn from their evil ways (Matthew 24:37-39). But who believes this today?

There was another who also prophesied that such times would come: a figure with a strong anti-Christian case. One can almost feel this figure haunting the scenes in "The Theater of Cruelty" — in plays where man is sold out to utter senselessness. We hear his voice in the background of numberless films, plays and books from all corners of the world which touch on this subject — the voice of Friedrich Nietzsche. He saw the devastation of mankind approaching. He prophesied that a chain of break-down, destruction, and revolution clanked at the door. The whole of European morality would collapse. Yet he himself helped bring it about. "Vital intoxication," he trumpeted, "that is the purpose of life." This principle of existence is best represented in the world of the Greek God, Dionysius. Nietzsche's being was captivated by a Dionysiac lust, a demonic intoxication which gives vent to all passions, and above all to sexual desire. In practicing this, he maintained, one's own self flows into the living stream of the universe. For a few moments one experiences the indestructible and eternal quality of sheer desire, with all its unrestrained thrust toward existence. In that moment one stands "beyond good and evil."

Europe, indeed the whole world, today is being more and more gripped by this Dionysiac life, this intoxication with lust and desire. And it follows a simple law of cause and effect: whoever takes narcotics, ends up by not being able to live without them. In a little poem, Nietzsche writes an appalling confession: "What lures Thee into the old Serpent's Paradise? . . . For now Thou art sick, sick with serpent's poison . . ."[34]

And now mankind, including youth — drinks this serpent's poison. And although it produces a delirium of delight, mankind becomes sick, for it is poison. Yet no one believes it. On the contrary, many publications, even some with a Christian viewpoint, do not have the courage to oppose this spirit of the age. Indeed, often it is excused — without recognizing that behind it stands the greater deceiver of mankind. The prince of this world, Lucifer, in these last days has set his mark upon mankind, to befuddle him with serpent guile, and then catapult him into destruction.

But one does wake from a state of delirium. The bliss of delirium is devilish, for on waking one finds himself filled with a haunting loneliness. Then comes the bitter aftertaste of desperation and emptiness, an aching void which nothing can fill. One stands soiled and guilty. Because one does not want to admit this, he seeks to push aside the uncomfortable feeling. But the only way open is the way of

---

[34] *Nietzsches Werke*, Kroenersche Klassikerausgabe, Volume 8, p. 145

further delusion — some new and yet stronger "narcotic," and thus one sinks deeper into the quagmire.

Therefore, whenever man wakens from his state of delirium today, he finds the world more chaotic, more puzzling, more impersonal and more senseless than before. It brings him close to insanity. The ecstatic excesses which dominated Nietzsche's last years brought him to insanity. During his years in the asylum, he actually believed he had become the god Dionysius. The French actor and director Artaud, the intellectual stimulus for the "Theater of Cruelty," also spent the last nine years of his life in an asylum.

Today millions stumble along in this state of delirium with its inevitable consequences. Life is lived in a dull stupor. Everything that happens is looked upon as "unavoidable destiny," and accepted as such. A fifteen-year-old English boy was asked what he would do if the four-minute warning for an atomic war sounded. "I'd go sleep with Brenda," he replied.[35]

A similar attitude is seen in the deafening applause given in February, 1964, to the film, "Dr. Strangelove, or: How I Learned to Stop Worrying and Love the Bomb." The film treats the danger of an atomic war with crass cynicism. Total annihilation, collective fear, and the reality of a death-machine are reduced to the level of macabre comedy. Revered values are ridiculed. The terror is resolved in utter frivolousness: The people watch the mushrooming of the deadly atomic cloud to the accompaniment of shallow pop music.[36]

That is one reaction to the insane situation of our time. Another is the ever-increasing suicide epidemic — an attempt to flee the cold, the senselessness, and the emptiness of today's world. In 1957 the number of suicides in West Ger-

---

[35]*FAZ*, March 8, 1964
[36]*Jedioth Chadaschoth*, February 1964

many almost equalled the deaths resulting from traffic accidents. If the number of unsuccessful attempts at suicide were added to this, the figure would considerably surpass the number of traffic deaths. And since then it has continued to rise steadily.

The Western world lives today under the sign of sexuality, brutality and the dissolution of all moral values. A veneer of Christianity may remain, but the majority of people have only a superficial knowledge of God. And this knowledge has no real connection with their life. Man no longer acknowledges God as LORD, nor His commandments as binding.

Up until now people in the Communist East have had a healthier attitude toward sexual morality than those in the West. But Western moral decadence is beginning to take its toll in these countries too.

In addition to this, the East is openly and avowedly atheistic. Its hate-slogans create an atmosphere of fear and dread, so that here also one lives in a state of continual uncertainty which leads to stupor. Here, too, murder and atrocity find their place, simply under other pretenses. The people are continually needled by atheistic agitation. In 1964 Moscow inaugurated an "Institute for Scientific Atheism." A festive opening celebration featured a large exhibition in which God was ridiculed in many ways.[37]

This spirit has already taken hold in East Germany, which lies behind the Iron Curtain. Is it not the voice of our time when one hears night club lyrics mocking God over the East German radio? Here is a sample —

> The Bible says:
> Long ago at the break of day
> God's own Son sped heavenward
> To His Father's throne.

---

[37] *FAZ*, February 3, 1964

> Since that day man waits
> For the Son of God to return.
> Today man is waiting still,
> But so far without any luck.
>
> TASS reports:
> For the first time, at the break of day
> A son of man flew heavenward
> From the Soviet Union!
>
> With your morning coffee tomorrow, TASS reports:
> Gagarin is back
> From his first ascension —
> Wishes us all luck!
>
> Many seek a paradise in heaven —
> But they forget
> That a paradise on earth
> Is much better for man!
>
> (literal translation from the German)

We indeed live in a time like none before. Our day bears the mark and characteristic of the end of time. But who believes it? Who, even in the Christian Church, believes it? Yet it is imperative that the Church does recognize it, for the Church has a mission from her Lord to sound the call of salvation. This is the call which has been entrusted to her for this hour in His Word. This is the day when the word of salvation must be lived out and shared abroad.

This call means a radical about-face. Christians must effect a complete separation from the evidences of decay in our time, before it is too late and we all perish.

The call to "turn and repent" is a call of glad tidings, "for the Kingdom of Heaven is at hand." And the more urgent this call, the closer at hand is the Kingdom of God. For a sign that the "great apostasy" has begun will be that "wickedness is multiplied" (Matthew 24:12). Jesus names this wickedness (literally, "lawlessness"), as one of the signs of the last days, and at the same time proclaims the nearness of His return. "They will see the Son of man coming on the clouds of heaven with power and great glory" (Matthew 24:30). But as it was in Jesus' time, so it is today: Even informed Christians do not recognize the signs of our times. Even a pure and simple reporting of facts they will label as "trying to make things too black and white." They do not recognize the urgency of this call to repentance.

Others, however, who do not even speak as representatives of the Christian community, face the facts squarely. In a book like *Where Do We Stand Today?*[38], well-known authors, scientists and artists portray the situation of our time from their viewpoint. Men of the most diverse professions make observations like the following:

"The moral condition of man, religion, and philosophy is tottering everywhere. It appears we are heading unchecked toward an unacknowledged nihilism which cloaks itself in rebellion, unbridled passion, intoxication, and fanaticism."[39] "We are being menaced by the collapse of a system of values which upholds our civilization, and on its heels a spiritual and moral vacuum which at best might be filled temporarily by a culture of materialistic stimulants, or some other substitute. The moral compass of mankind has lost its sense of direction."[40]

When responsible men from various professions and points of view portray our time as a "spiritual and moral vacuum," one must take heed: We stand on the brink of the abyss. What a shame that this clear call does not come from the Christian Church in our day. Yet it is typical of the time preceding a downfall that no one believes it. Consider the Biblical case of Sodom and Gomorrah and that of the Great Flood.

---
[38] Baehr, *Wo Stehen wir heute?* Bertelsmann-Verlag 1961
[39] Op. cit., p. 41
[40] Op. cit., p. 74

Is there yet help for us? Yes, we must heed the voice of God. We must heed His Word. We must make a clean break with the perverse and godless existence which surrounds us. Our stand must be clear and unequivocal. For the Lord tells us that for men — and especially Christians — who live a life of adultery, fornication, immorality and debauchery, the door of God's Kingdom remains closed (Galatians 5:19-21; Ephesians 5:5). He says that the wrath of God will come upon the disobedient — those who indulge in "immorality, impurity, passion, evil desires" (Ephesians 5:6; Colossians 3:5, 6). By living thus in the filth of immorality, defiling passion, shamelessness, and twisted ideas, men are storing up for themselves wrath on the day when the righteous judgment of God will be revealed. Tribulation and distress will come for every human being who does evil (Romans 1:24-31; 2:5, 9). This is what the living God says to us in His Word.

What a fearful judgment awaits men and women who so live — especially those who reckon themselves baptized members of the Christian Church. The wrath of God is stored up against the world. His sword of judgment is poised above us. Unless we take an uncompromising stand against such sinful ways, we will have no power to oppose the evil of our day, which entices man with its seductive call as never before. Above all, we will lack the power to warn others with convincing authority of the danger of this seduction, and rescue them from destruction. Those who take God's Word seriously must sound the alarm.

But our situation today is exactly as it was in the time of Noah: Those who speak of the "judgment of God" are only laughed at and ridiculed. Who has the manly courage to stand up and call sin and guilt by their proper names? Yet, can obedience to God's Word and love for one's fellow men tolerate anything less? But what do we see? Instead, in Christian circles we hear frequently about the "unholiness of the world," on the one hand and on the other about "compassion for one's fellow man." But God is waiting today for men who will call sin *sin*. Sin is something so horrible to God that Jesus had to suffer death on the cross because of it. God waits today for those who will sound the call to repentance, and by the same token the call to salvation in Jesus, the Saviour.

Yet this call alone will not suffice. Our witness and our life go together. It is not enough to merely call people to a life of purity and discipline: Our own lives must provide an example of these same qualities. We must give ourselves to purity and disciplined Christian living with a passion. Today mankind languishes in the grip of demonic powers. He gives himself with passion to unrestrained sexuality and every base desire. The passion of the Christian for purity and righteousness must not be a whit less. The love between man and woman, in marriage, must regain its godly and noble character. Marriages must again be ordered according to the divine pattern which God established when He ordained marriage as a divine institution. The Word of God must again become binding. And according to the Word of God adultery is a sin, and marriage cannot be broken except in the case of unchastity by one of the partners (Matthew 5:32). Today, as never before, we must lay hold on every commandment of God, every wise counsel of Scripture, with a faith that is deadly earnest. For in no other way can the will of God be fulfilled.

Mankind stands on the brink of catastrophe. A weak, half-hearted call will not be heeded. Only the witness of our *life* will have the power to penetrate man's stupor. It cannot be accomplished with endless "objective discussions" of the questions which concern us. No one can say, "*Am* I my brother's keeper?" Every disciple of Jesus, every one who knows the commandments of God, is under obligation today to sound the alarm. And how does one "sound the alarm"? Through the witness of one's life, through books, through articles, through tracts which one gives out to those closest at hand: fellow workers, friends, one's own family. For every Christian should be a missionary. And this means, above all, to help and to rescue the imperiled, according to Jesus' commandment of love. Today influences of a truly demonic nature envelop mankind in a cloud of stupor and befuddlement. Through the medium of movies, theater, literature, and television this spirit of our time is spread abroad. The great mass of mankind has succumbed to it. Who can blithely "pass by on the other side"? Who can without pang of conscience give them up not only to despair, sin, guilt, and suicide, but to a condemned existence through all eternity in the Kingdom of Torment? And so the call is clear: "Do thou likewise!" — Do all that you can to save any who will be saved. Whoever fails to do what he can in this desperate hour will bear a guilt for these lost souls, and especially those of the youth.

But if our help is to be practical and effective, we must ourselves be clear about the philosophical causes which have led to the demoralization.

CAUSES IN THE REALM OF THE HISTORY OF HUMAN INTELLECT DURING THE PAST TWO CENTURIES:

THE ENTIRE CIVILIZED WORLD has been deeply impregnated with Christian ideas. Yet today this same civilized world is a study in demoralization, as we have seen. How did this come to pass?

In the West and in the East ethical values have been upset. Mankind lives by the watchwords of hate and godlessness. How are we to understand this? How have we arrived at this state of nihilism, where whim and passion are given free rein? Have advances in science and technology fashioned this mood in our day? Is it simply an inevitable historical development? Do we see in our day the culmination of a long process of development, the inevitable result of a clear and discernible cause?

Indeed, this is precisely what we see. In 1762 a message was proclaimed to the educated world of that day. The ground for it had been prepared by English and French philosophy since the beginning of the century. What a glad message it seemed to be! It proclaimed freedom, justice and the dignity of man! This philosophical impulse came from the French author and philosopher Rousseau, in his book *Social Contract*. He made a "Copernican discovery" in the realm of philosophy. In the 16th Century Copernicus had effected a change in man's conception of the physical universe through his discovery that the sun, rather than the earth, is the center of the solar system. Now, according to Rousseau, *the human spirit must no longer orbit around God as a center, but around mankind itself.* To be sure, at first this came out in Rousseau only indistinctly, in the framework of his "religion of feeling." But others took up the theme, urging him to formulate a clear challenge. Yes, said Rousseau, man must completely re-orient his processes of reason and thinking. When he does, a new society will emerge, an ideal society, a paradise on earth.

The shift of emphasis was subtle. For many it passes altogether unnoticed. Yet with this re-orientation Rousseau shifted the center around which everything, including the human spirit, had revolved until then. This center had always been God. Until this time God was the Final Authority; He was, indeed, the LORD. What God willed and commanded was recognized. He had made it clearly known in the Ten Commandments. This was the foundation of ethics. Until then men, by and large, felt dependent upon God. In general, man saw himself, with his sin and guilt, subordinated to God: God was the Final Judge, who could condemn him or grant him mercy.

Now Rousseau "discovered" that man is "by nature free and good." And therefore mankind, thanks to the human intellect (which is identical with man's good nature), can make its own laws, as an expression of the common will. The laws which men thus establish Rousseau held to be "absolute," "holy," and "inviolable."

"You shall be like God. You shall determine for yourself what is good and what is evil!" Yes, the poison of the Serpent, at work since the beginning of human history, had penetrated unnoticed at a crucial point. God was dethroned, and mankind usurped the throne.

The seed of this was scattered abroad through the French Revolution. But part of the guilt must be borne by the Church. In the eighteenth century many of the clergy lorded it over man's conscience intolerantly, even though unbelief was rife in their own ranks. The flame of love burned low. The Church neglected her social tasks. The low moral level of representatives of the Church tended to encourage the opposition of those who were sympathetic with the spirit of the revolution. In France the people languished under a despotic monarchy. And no little cause for this lay in the union between "throne and altar." All of this helped to conjure up what began with the French Revolution. And so a Christianity, often a poor caricature of what it should be, her conduct often a slap in the face and a discredit to the Gospel, helped precipitate the French Revolution and its revolutionary ideas.

We in the Church of Jesus Christ must first of all face our own guilt, which touched off the beginning of the revolt against God in the Age of the Enlightenment. In the ensuing centuries this revolt has moved out in ever-widening circles, with ever-increasing effect. Today the ideology of the French

Revolution has become the working principle of a mankind which has lost its moorings in the area of faith and morals.

The Enlightenment of Rousseau's time included belief in a supernatural God who created the world and the laws of nature. This conception of God was known as Deism. But the God of the Bible was set aside. For man no longer believed that God still revealed Himself to men, that He entered into personal relationship with men, that He spoke to men. One no longer believed that God dealt concretely with him, or with nations, or that He intervened in human history. In short, man no longer believed that God loved men, and wanted their love in return. And so the First Commandment was summarily set aside.

A new self-consciousness had become awakened. Man himself now became the measure of all things. Pointing to himself with pride, as though he himself had newly discovered human intelligence, man spoke of "Light," which has the characteristics of the divine *Logos*. And through this "Light" of human intelligence man could also see the way to making badly needed improvements in social conditions.

And what was the consequence of this line of reasoning? Consider the following: In the French Revolution man did not shy away even from "Putting God on Trial." According to Hazard, the French literary historian, the charges read: "The God of the Christians had had all power and had used it poorly. Man had trusted Him, and He had deceived man. . . . according to the rules of logic and our understanding, the plan of divine providence was altogether lacking in inner coherence."[41]

Here one sees the real motive for this upheaval in the world of thought and reason: It was unbelief, which is not in

---

[41] Paul Hazard *Die Herrschaft der Vernunft das europaeische Denken im 18. Jahrhundert,* translated from the French by Harriet Wegener and Karl Linnebach, 1949, p. 88f

the first place a matter of understanding, but a matter of the heart remonstrating and rebelling against God. The heart rebels against God because it senses that it is dependent on God. The French philosopher Holbach speaks openly about this. He protests against the "divine despotism." Against this he "thunders vehemently" and "flings curses."[42] When man fashions a world governed by his own reason, God becomes a disturbance. In such a world there is no place for a God to whose absolute will one must submit in all things.

This was the end result of Rousseau's "religion of feeling." He himself did not want to become an atheist. But he drank the Serpent's poison: "You shall be like God." He set up human intelligence as the highest moral authority. And so reason became a substitute for God. The end of it all was the open rebellion against God in the French Revolution.

Such poison brings with it a kind of intoxication. In the initial stages of this intoxication, one dreamed of an earthly paradise, a new order created by a return to the ideal conditions of nature — a "Kingdom of God," of sorts. But when one woke from the dream, the stark reality of the poison's effect revealed itself. The Republic of the Guillotine did not bring freedom: It brought unending oppression. It did not bring forth the dignity of man: It brought crime. It did not bring paradise-like conditions: It brought destruction and death. The first attempt to shift the center of faith in man's life from God to man had a negative outcome. It became evident that faith and morals are inseparably bound together. Man had set his faith on something false, namely on the "essential goodness of man." And this false faith had its outcome. The unbridled passions and sinful desires of the French Revolution led to an insane theater of horror and a dreadful bloodbath. And afterward the general moral tone of life in France continued to decline.

---

[42] G. W. Plechanow *Beitraege zur Geschichte des Materialismus* 1922, p. 31-40

Rousseau surely did not foresee that his new teaching would lead to warfare between man and the living God and Lord. Yet it did, and the end of it was a monstrous defeat for man. The Word of God had proved true: "The imagination of man's heart is evil from his youth" (Genesis 8:21). God showed that He is still the living God, and the Judge of mankind. He will punish and discipline those who rise up against Him, who set up their own laws, who set aside the commandments of God, and attempt to set up their own "Kingdom of God" on earth.

The French Revolution placed man, rather than God, at the center. As an experiment it failed. Yet with it the avalanche had begun to move. The dethronement of God had been fully effected at the spiritual level. And even though no one believed it, this stood in direct relation to the hell of the guillotine. In the period following, this initial revolt against God developed into a protracted rebellion. And, as one would expect, a revolution in morals and ethics followed in its train.

One can trace a clear development in man's philosophical and intellectual history over these past two centuries: It began with the French Revolution and the Age of the Enlightenment; it has led in the West to nihilism, and in the East to communism. Karl Marx, the great atheist and God-hater, was therefore quite right when he pointed to the French Revolution and rationalism as the most important turning point in the development of mankind up to that time.

What stages have we passed through in these two centuries? We select a few names — highly gifted personalities who embodied and expressed the spirit of their time. These men took the themes and slogans of their times, systematically developed them, and passed them on to the people. They are the German philosophers Kant, Fichte, Hegel, and Feuerbach. In their writings this theme of the "autonomous, self-determined man" came out with greater and greater force.

Today the effect of this intellectual revolution can hardly be gainsaid. The daily existence of man, both in the East and the West, is thoroughly stamped and impregnated with it.

Kant's immediate concern as such was to rediscover "faith in God." He sought in his own way to meet the challenge of the Enlightenment. In doing so, however, he reduced religion to a moral code. According to Kant, the business of religion is simply to challenge the moral disposition of man. Religious acts as such — prayer, worship, devotion, adoration — are denied, or become merely symbolic forms. A personal relationship to God is highly questionable. According to Kant, "wishing to please the Almighty" is a cringing, unworthy attempt to flatter oneself. Prayer is superstition and fetishism. Kant virtually denied any specific obligation of man toward God. For him, Christianity is "the idea of religion, which is based purely on reason, and therefore, is merely 'natural.' "[43] Scarcely anyone guessed — or wanted to believe — that these ideas of Kant would cause the avalanche to roll further, yet that is what happened. And in the period following, the representatives of German idealism gave the avalanche another mighty push.

This new wave came from the young theologians in Tubingen, where Schelling and Hegel, together with Hoelderin, spent their student years at the turn of the nineteenth century. With their roots and background in the area of Christian theology, they were able to exert a tremendous influence upon theological thinking. They took up the call of Rousseau: "Man, by nature, has inalienable rights. The spirit of man is free." It had a heady effect on the young Tubingen theologians. Like Rousseau, they saw the "end times" approaching, and the Kingdom of God coming on earth. But their conception of the Kingdom of God was false: They saw it merely in terms of rising standards of living and improved social

---

[43] Kant *Der Streit der Fakultaeten*, published by K. Rossmann 1947, p. 67

conditions. The "childhood" of the human race was past, with its restrictions and limitations. Schelling spoke of "Almighty Man";[44] and Hegel wrote, "the primary idea is the conception of myself as an absolutely free being."[45]

The battle line was thus drawn between the reigning theology and a personal faith in God. Strife was inevitable. The poison spread like a cancer through the thought world of German Idealism. Hegel actually did not want to become an atheist. But he grimly resisted the divine demand that man owes God obedience and love. The practical result was that God was politely bowed off the stage of human affairs, so that nothing would stand in the way of human freedom. Man was to be the unchallenged master of his own newly-discovered greatness. God was merely an object for speculation. So even though Hegel's work, to begin with, had some of the outward form and trappings of Christianity, he was actually the forerunner of a thorough-going atheism — and incidentally also of nihilism, for he was the first one to speak about the "uncanny power of the negative," which was a decisive factor for him.[46] The idealism of Hegel is the source of modern atheism. Hegel is the proof of a basic spiritual principle: Where the living God, with His claims upon us, is no longer regarded, atheism takes over.

In the place of a personal God, Hegel substituted "destiny." "Destiny" was the ordering power of the universe. Evil, as such, is rendered relatively harmless. For in Hegel's system, history advances toward its goal through a series of dialectical encounters between good and evil, and therefore evil is no longer absolutely evil. This led to yet a further revolution in the realm of ethics.

But who saw the full implications of Hegel's thought in those heady days of German idealism? Scarcely anyone would

---
[44]*Epikureisch Glaubensbekenntnis Heinz Widerporstens*
[45]Joh. Hoffmeister *Dokumente zu Hegels Entwicklung*, 1936, p. 219
[46]Robert Heiss "Die Magie des Nichts," *FAZ*, April 4, 1964

have guessed that later the movement of godlessness would hark back to Hegel; especially when Hegel himself, in his later years, found his way back to a faith in God. So the avalanche rolled on: From theology as the study of God, to speculative philosophy as a philosophy of pure reason, on to anthropology as the study of man . . . man, around whom everything now revolved.

Anthropology was Feuerbach's special field of study. It came to have a determinative influence in the second half of the nineteenth century. For Kant, the power of "absolute reason" had occupied the focal position. Lofty and detached, it provided the basis for a morality which man must strive to fulfill. Feuerbach advanced a step further, and put man himself in the center: Man, just as he is, with all his natural qualities and tendencies, becomes the focal point of all human reckoning. Up until now, the question of God — whether He exists or not — occupied the philosophers. Now man had come so far that the question was scarcely relevant. One observed it, in passing, as an interesting historical curiosity. According to Feuerbach, the question of God belonged to the seventeenth and eighteenth centuries, but no longer to the nineteenth century.[47] For it had been established that God is not a reality. "For man, man himself is God." The avalanche gathers force as it tumbles toward its rendezvous in the valley, where it will wreak its havoc.

Like a huge boulder joining an avalanche, it was then Nietzsche who gave the final impetus to this hurtling destruction. The "pious atheism" of Feuerbach still had a tinge of religion about it. Nietzsche outpaced all this with his prophetic pronouncement: "God is dead!" This laid the groundwork for the thorough-going revolutionary doctrine of a Karl Marx. The godless movement which Karl Marx fostered honors Nietzsche as its "star witness." In Nietzsche one

---

[47] *Ludwig Feuerbach*: *Saemtliche Werke,* Bolin and Jodl 1903-1911, Vo. 2. p. 411

sees an incarnation of the legendary figure of Prometheus, the demi-god of Greek mythology who rebelled against the gods. Prometheus has become an ideal for modern man, who raises himself against God in arrogant, presumptuous rebellion. Indeed, modern man fancies himself in the role of Prometheus: "My proud temper can not bear to have the gods wield the scepter . . . for me, naught but the glory of the magnificent deed!" So wrote the youthful Nietzsche — a starting self-revelation — in his drama *Prometheus*. In Schelling and Hegel one saw the ideas of the "superman" in germinal form. They alluded to it as an ideal. With Nietzsche the idea actually came to birth, and with it the avalanche pitches headlong into the valley. The foundations of faith in God, and therewith also the basis for ethics, were destroyed. An existence "beyond good and evil" was proclaimed.

And such indeed is the life of a great cross-section of mankind today. This revolutionary development in philosophy at first took place merely in the realm of thought. It moved more-or-less outside the great mass of people, not greatly affecting their everyday life.

The appearance of Karl Marx on the scene marked a decisive turning point. Marx sought to transfer an atheistic orientation from the sphere of thought to the sphere of political practice. With his "Communist Manifesto" he wanted to bring a revolutionary New Thing into the course of human history. And indeed his works did go beyond the border of speculative philosophy, to exert a phenomenal influence on the political life of the world. He saw himself as a Master Architect, called to rebuild and reshape the world, changing and renewing whole peoples. And he would do it as a Prometheus, as a mighty Titan. In the Preface to his dissertation Marx wrote: "The Creed of Prometheus: 'In a word, I utterly hate each and every god!' This is philosophy's creed, the only word we address to all heavenly and earthly gods, who do not regard human self-consciousness as the highest deity."[48] For Karl Marx, this kind of atheism was the instrument for seizing entire nations, in which this atheism should then become a mass phenomenon. For the spirit seeks concrete manifestation. It cannot rest until it has stamped its imprint upon peoples and nations. The French Revolution attempted to build an earthly paradise based on Rousseau's book, *Social Contract*. With Karl Marx, the attempt was repeated on a gigantic scale.

With these political programs Marx — and later Engels — did not hark back only to the French Revolution. They also drew heavily on classical philosophy: "The German Workers' Movement is the heir of German classical philosophy."[49] "We German Socialists are proud to trace our lineage not only from Saint Simon, Fourier, and Owen, but also from Kant, Fichte, and Hegel."[50] Karl Marx admitted freely his intellectual debt to Hegel and Feuerbach.

Lenin's ideas stem from the same source. He, too, was proud to think of himself as the true heir of German dialectical philosophy — the courageous executor of Hegel's will and testament. He expected his fellow workers to study Hegel's theory of dialectic systematically. Through the dialectic encounter of opposites, Hegel's teaching sought to bring to light the true nature of things. And thanks to this teaching, according to Lenin, hundreds of millions of people all over the world have been wakened from their slumber. What frightening results a seemingly harmless twisting of creed can have! These changes in the realm of belief brought

---

[48] *Karl Marx-Friedrich Engels*: Hist. Kritische Gesamtausgabe 1927, Volume I, 1, 1; p. 9f.
[49] Engels: *Ludwig Feuerbach und der Ausgang der klassischen deutschen Philosophie,* Neuausgabe Berlin 1946, p. 53
[50] Engels: *Die Entwicklung des Sozialismus von der Utopie zur Wissenschaft* 1882, Neuausgabe Berlin 1951, p. 5

world-wide repercussions and altered the destinies of whole peoples. At the time no one suspected it. Yet it lay in the very nature of the case.

Popularized by Marx and Lenin, these ideas began to find concrete historical expression. In the sense that it was a social experiment, it bore certain resemblances to the French Revolution. But it went beyond that. In the wake of the French Revolution came many injustices and atrocities. These were plain for all to see. They played, as it were, on a public stage. But that was now changed. The result of later attempts would no longer be displayed so openly. As the spirit of the Antichrist gets stronger and stronger, the spirit of deception also becomes stronger. Behind it is the spirit of Satan, the opponent of God, who is a liar from the beginning. Today where we find atheism being used as an intellectual means for accomplishing political objectives in the Marxian sense, we also find propaganda which often conceals the true conditions.

But facts speak louder than all the propaganda. The lands under the sway of Marxism proclaim freedom. Yet in these lands millions of people live out their lives more or less fettered in mind and spirit. They have no freedom to voice a belief or philosophy of their own. They live for the most part in a compulsory labor system. Some are consigned to the degrading life of the prison and the concentration camp. "Freedom" wears the chains of slavery. "Paradise on earth" betrays the characteristics of hell. The heralded "paradise of prosperity" more often resembles a kingdom of misery, for thousands go hungry, suffer want, and live in poverty. Millions of people live in a "Kingdom of Peace" — where the military upbringing begins in grammar school. In this touted "Kingdom of Blessing," millions of people actually live in an empire of terror — because it is an empire of unleashed hatred against God. Such hate kills, demoralizes, destroys.

And in the West? Here the "Experiment of Revolting Against God" has a somewhat different character. It is not promulgated with such single-minded and systematic determination as in the East. But here, too, Nietzsche has reached his goal. He is not only the star witness for atheism, but also for its twin, which characterizes the West — nihilism. Life today portrays precisely what Nietzsche prophesied: "What I say concerning the advent of nihilism will become the history of the next two centuries. I describe what is coming, for nothing else can come. Our entire European culture has been writhing in tension for a long time. The situation changes now from decade to decade. A catastrophe seems to impend. The air is uneasy, charged with power, precarious. A pressure is building up, like a geyser ready to erupt, and it can no longer reflect and consider — it is afraid any longer to reflect and consider."[51]

This word has become a reality in our own day. Nihilism holds sway not only in the West, but more and more over the whole world. The Tree of Knowledge has borne its fruit, and spread out over the whole earth. Another of Nietzsche's prophetic utterances has become equally true: In East and West the "Eclipse of Gloom" has begun, for "we have killed the gods." "But," Nietzsche continues, "what did we do when we cut this earth loose from her sun? Where is the earth headed now? Where are we headed? Are we headed away from all suns? Are we not stumbling all the while backward, sideward, forward, in every direction? Is there still 'Up' and 'Down'? Do we not go astray with this endless 'Nothing'? Is not this great emptiness oppressive?"[52]

Mocking, as a voice from the grave, come the prophetic words of Nietzsche to our ears today: "God is dead!" They shrill out over the millions of people in the East subjected to a movement which is dominated by a fanatical spirit of

---
[51] Robert Heiss "Die Magie des Nichts," op. cit.
[52] *Nietzsches Werke, Kroeners Klassikerausgabe,* Volume 5, p. 163f.

godlessness. And no less do these words mock the millions in the West who watch the films, plays, and advertisements impregnated by the same spirit. People give themselves over to the intoxication of sex, brutality, narcotics and thrills. They feel drawn into a yawning abyss — given over to their sins. Why? "Because although they knew God they did not honor him as God or give thanks to him, but they became futile in their thinking and their senseless minds were darkened. Therefore God gave them up in the lusts of their hearts to impurity, to the dishonoring of their bodies among themselves" (Romans 1:21, 24).

The Bible speaks with unmistakable clarity: Because God is no longer honored, because He no longer holds first place in our thoughts, our love, our life — but instead the "senseless mind of man" has usurped His place — therefore comes the breakdown of morality which we are witnessing today. But no one wants to believe that this alone is the reason for today's moral landslide. True, one can cite many other factors which have contributed to this breakdown — such as the failures of the Church, social injustice, and others as well. Nevertheless, the only valid judgment as to the cause and effect of immorality among men is the judgment God Himself sets forth in the Bible. His words are straightforward and to the point: "Since they did not see fit to acknowledge God, God gave them up to a base mind and improper conduct" (Romans 1:28). Here is where a 180-degree reversal of our thinking must take place. That is the commandment of the hour for our churches, and our theology. Does the Church believe the word of Scripture — and will she act accordingly?

CAUSES IN THE REALM OF THEOLOGY

"Our image of God must go!"

With this arresting title, *The Observer* in March, 1963 announced a new book by an Anglican Bishop, *Honest to*

God.[53] This well-publicized book was sold out within a few hours of its release. It has since become one of the most widely-sold books in the Christian world, with more than 400,000 copies already in print. Eight foreign-language editions are either in print or under consideration.

The author of the book, Bishop John A. T. Robinson, admits that his interpretation amounts to an intellectual and spiritual revolution. The Biblical concept of God which we have held up until now, based on the Old and New Testaments, must disappear. "In fact the coming of the space age has destroyed this crude projection of God — and for that we should be grateful."[54] The revolution begins with the statement that outside the reality surrounding us there is no God. "The word 'God' denotes the ultimate depth for all our being, the creative ground and meaning of all our existence. So conditioned for us is the word 'God' by associations with a Being out there that Tillich warns us that to make the necessary transposition, 'you must forget everything traditional that you have learned about God, perhaps even that word itself.' "[55]

Is it really true, as many reports about Bishop Robinson's book say, that hitherto valid religious terminology is being replaced by a "non-religious but faithful and unabridged existential language"? Is Christian theology and proclamation here merely seeking the right language with which to bring the Gospel of Jesus Christ to modern man in our world of atomic power, technology and space travel?

Certainly Robinson takes great pains to translate the language of the New Testament into the language of today. He wants at all costs to make it understandable in terms of man's life today. But his painstaking effort is a far cry from that of the Apostle Paul. Paul became a Jew to the Jews and a

---
[53] *The Observer* March 1963
[54] Robinson, *Honest to God,* S.C.M Press, 1963, p. 14
[55] Robinson, op. cit., p. 47

Greek to the Greeks. But in so doing he only intensified his preaching of the cross of Christ. There was no abridgement of the basic message. On the contrary, his proclamation was so absolute and "in the power of God" (the Greek word here, "dynamis," is the root of our word "dynamite"!) that his preaching was a "stumbling block to the Jews and foolishness to the Greeks" (I Corinthians 1:23). Robinson wants to "translate" the Christian message from its Biblical language into a modern idiom. But in so doing he runs this danger: For the sake of "modern man," he adapts and actually alters the content of the message. For when he speaks of "God," it is no longer the living God who reveals Himself in the Bible. It is rather the "Ground of Being," which in the final analysis restricts it to the realm of man. Thus the Christian faith is whittled down to size, well within the grasp of man, and owning no character of a revealed truth.

Robinson's book is actually a popularization of several streams of theological thought. It draws, for instance, upon the results of the "de-mythologizing school" in Germany: "It is impossible to switch on an electric light or a radio, and at the same time believe in the world of spirits and miracles which one encounters in the New Testament."[56] Robinson also draws on the theology of Paul Tillich, from which he borrows the concept of God as the "Ground of Being." He also makes reference to Bonhoeffer, though he apparently misunderstands him.

In all of this, the question of "human existence" occupies the front-ranking position. Robinson wants to break loose from a dead orthodoxy — a worthy motive. He seeks to offer man a vital religious experience within the framework of human existence as such. But in so doing, he calls into question the possibility and the reality of an actual encounter

---

[56]R. Bultmann, *Kerygma und Mythos,* vol. 1, p. 18

with the living God. And this puts man in a dangerous position: His religious experience centers in himself; he is no longer dependent on God, is no longer His creature. Now man, "modern man," sets the standards. What can we accept in the Bible? Ask modern man. Which moral imperatives in the Bible are still binding? Ask modern man. In a convulsive attempt to "make contact with modern man," one loses contact with God, from whom all things — including "modern man" — come.

This comes out clearly when Robinson rebels against the core of the New Testament message: "Much indeed of this mythological drama — such as the ransom paid to the Devil or the notion that the Father punishes the Son in our place — is in any case a perversion of what the New Testament says. But, even when it is Christian in content, the whole schema of a supernatural Being coming down from heaven to 'save' mankind from sin, in the way that a man might put his finger into a glass of water to rescue a struggling insect, is frankly incredible to man 'come of age,' who no longer believes in such a deus ex machina, insofar as the content of this conception is even Christian."[57] Here Robinson draws upon the de-mythologizing school of theology. The story of a God-man who atones for the sins of mankind with his blood is treated as a myth or saga.

And what does he make of the Christmas story? "Jesus was not a man born and bred — he was God for a limited period taking part in a charade. He looked like a man, he talked like a man, he felt like a man, but underneath he was God dressed up — like Father Christmas. However guardedly it may be stated, the traditional view leaves the impression that God took a space-trip and arrived on this planet in the form of a man. Jesus was not really one of us; but through the miracle of the Virgin Birth he contrived to be born so as to

---

[57] Robinson, op. cit., p. 78.

appear one of us. . . . But suppose the whole notion of 'a God' who 'visits' the earth in the person of 'his Son' is as mythical as the prince in the fairy story? Suppose there is no realm 'out there' from which the 'Man from heaven' arrives? Suppose the Christmas myth (the invasion of 'this side' by 'the other side') — as opposed to the Christmas history (the birth of the man Jesus of Nazareth) — has to go? Are we prepared for that? Oh, it can remain (this supernatural schema of thought) — but only as myth."[58]

In other words, it is a religious fairy tale! Nor are these assertions moderated by the author's admission: "I am aware that this is a parody, and probably an offensive one, but I think it is perilously near the truth of what most people — and I would include myself — have been brought up to believe at Christmas time."[59]

Countless readers have chorused their approval of Robinson's statements, and some of this has come from circles of real believers. In many lands, the book has had an astonishing effect within the Christian Church. One cannot simply overlook this. It is a symptom of some of the religious influences which are at work beneath the surface in the Christian Church today. The readers find their own thoughts confirmed in what Robinson says. They rejoice at last to have found someone who has the courage to speak the truth. And they sense in addition the admittedly sincere personal concern of Robinson to bring the message of the Bible closer to modern man.

But in all of this, it is no new truth which is being proclaimed. The Age of Rationalism and Idealism trumpeted the same message: "The old conception of God must go!" And this was long before "modern man" came on the scene. The great discoveries of natural science and technology were not even in the picture. No, the neo-rationalism of

---
[58] Robinson, op. cit., p. 67
[59] Robinson, op. cit., p. 66

Robinson does not offer us anything new. It merely brings *into the realm of theology* certain thoughts of the past which have become current in present-day atheistic philosophy.

On the other hand, the latest achievements of natural science have actually paved the way for the Christian faith — if indeed it needed such! The conclusions of nineteenth century natural science were based on a rigid materialistic concept. It left no room for the supernatural or the miraculous. But these conclusions no longer stand. Max Planck's Quantum Theory and Albert Einstein's Theory of Relativity have fashioned radically new concepts in the natural sciences. Robinson himself states that on the basis of these discoveries, "Nothing should hinder us from once again locating God beyond the outer limits of space." But then he comes to some oddly contrary conclusions.[60]

But the point is this: The latest discoveries of natural science and the advances in technology no longer provide a comfortable basis for rejecting faith in the living God. At one time science spoke confidently of "absolute space" and "absolute time." Now these conceptions have had to be overhauled, which simply illustrates the fact that scientific statements are never eternally valid. Therefore no theology can accept the statements of natural science as a point of departure. Science can never be called as a "star witness" to validate the claims of faith. Scientific conclusions are subject to constant revision. When a theory is disproved by further research, it is discarded. Science can only state what it understands or seems to understand at any given time. The statements of faith, on the other hand, claim eternal validity. This does not mean that faith's conception of God is rigid and static. For faith speaks of a God who reveals Himself, who acts and performs miracles. . .yesterday, today, and forever!

---

[60]Robinson, op. cit., p. 14

So it is not the discoveries of science which have shaken the foundations of faith — faith in a God who works miracles, faith in the resurrection as literal happening. Rather, this erosion of faith has come about because of the attitude of our hearts. One thing that the Age of the Enlightenment did bring to light was the fact that we human beings cannot bear to live under One who is Lord and Judge. So "let's get rid of our conception of God!" — the living God who reveals Himself as Lord, Creator and Judge. For then man himself will be lord. Then man will be truly free. Then man will be independent of God, and of His judgments. And as "lord" he will no longer need a Redeemer.

But this kind of "freedom" brings frightful results. When a man no longer needs a Saviour from sin, he no longer has regard for the Ten Commandments, which point out his sin. Thus the foundation of morality gives way — and this time at the very center, that is, in the Christian Church itself. Such a "revolution in ethics" should be an alarm signal to us, indicating the times in which we live.

"Today," Robinson says, "the absolute demands (by this he means the commandments given by God) are presented to us stripped of their mythological garb. The mighty event of Sinai has lost its terror. Jesus also has lost his authority, even as a great moral teacher."[61] Such statements betoken nothing less than a deep rebellion of the heart against the living God and His will, as revealed in His commandments.

Here we see coming to pass what no one wants to believe. When God is no longer at the center, when He is no longer reverenced, ethical standards collapse: The moral landslide has begun. It is no coincidence that an attack on the commandments of Sinai should go hand in hand with the campaign of a society to reform the laws on homosexuality.[62]

---
[61]Robinson, op. cit., p. 106-109
[62]*Evang. Kirchenzeitung,* August 6, 1964

There are deep and significant connections here: Moral foundations begin to crumble whenever we presume to meddle with the Sinai commandments. God alone is Lord and Lawgiver. Human standards can never replace His divine commands. And therefore the present moral landslide, which is heading mankind for destruction, is doubly frightening. For it is not supported merely by "free thinkers," but by leaders within the Christian Church. This shows us the lateness of the hour. Midnight is fast approaching.

Yet many who read this book of Robinson's do not want to believe it. "This so-called 'ethical revolution'," they say, "is nothing at all like what took place in the Enlightenment and the French Revolution. This is a *Christian* movement." This is precisely the danger and that which leads many astray! The Apostles John and Paul set forth love as the highest commandment. But there was an overriding qualification: It was love *bound to God and proceeding from Him*. In the new theology too, "love" is used as a touchstone for ethics, but in a misleading way: It is not bound to God, the living Creator and Judge of mankind. We read: "Nothing can of itself always be labelled as 'wrong.' One cannot, for instance, start from the position 'sex relations before marriage' or 'divorce' are wrong or sinful in themselves. . .the only intrinsic evil is lack of love. . .nothing else makes a thing right or wrong."[63]

But Jesus teaches differently: "Every one who divorces his wife and marries another commits adultery" (Luke 16:18). And in the preceding verse, a superscription, as it were, to the commandment against divorce: "It is easier for heaven and earth to pass away, than for one dot of the law to become void" (Luke 16:17).

In contrast to this, man now determines what may be done and allowed. He takes "love" as a standard. But it

---

[63]Robinson, op. cit., p. 118-119

is a love no longer bound to God. It is a fallen, fettered, and often degenerate love. Such human "love" cannot lead us with certainty to right ethical decisions. Indeed, the devilish reverse can often be the case. We saw that happen in Adolph Hitler's regime. He professed a great "love" for his German people. He wanted to "protect them from inferior groups." And so, out of "love," six million Jews — including more than a million children — were murdered in the cruelest way. Out of "love" to his people, in order to free them from "unnecessary burdens" an end was put to hundreds of thousands of weak and so-called worthless lives. In 1964 the great euthanasia trial was held, where these deeds were to be judged. And still, after twenty years, the chief defendant maintained that his motive was purely "love for mankind" and "compassion." In his closing statement he said: "I saw it all from a purely ethical point of view."[64] This is what one comes to when man becomes the measure of things, rather than God and what He says in His Word. Then even murder becomes permissible, in the name of "love."

It is a great self-deception to suppose that the human heart is "basically good." The human heart is the dwelling place of jealousy, envy, egotism, hate and bitterness. No one can make right decisions purely on the basis of "love." The love must be born of God, and bound to His commandments. No one — not even the man with the highest ethical standards — can always recognize evil and really overcome it of his own accord.

How then are we to understand the excited acclaim which *Honest to God* has received from so many Christians? From England it has gone into the whole world as the "new teaching." As in the time of Paul, it "eats its way like gangrene" (II Timothy 2:17). How can this be? Robinson's point of view is not restricted to the Anglican Church, nor even to

---

[64]*FAZ*, March 3, 1964

Protestantism. Teachers in the Roman Catholic Church who espouse his views have also gained a wide hearing. A leading Catholic publication wrote: "In Robinson's book one senses a genuine Christian attitude. He is not satisfied merely to hold an established position and protect the faithful. He has a real missionary impulse."[65]

How are we to understand that in Anglican and Protestant circles, as well as in the Catholic world, so many do not believe that here powers from below are at work? These powers will not rest until the poison of demoralization, immorality, and lawlessness which dwells in mankind has penetrated right into the heart of the Church. When this happens, the last dam will have broken. What is the reason for this blindness in the Church of Jesus Christ? Why her uncertain wavering behavior? For thereby she actually hastens the "hour of gloom" which Nietzsche prophesied.

The English bishop says that the old conceptions of God, traditional Christianity, must be set aside. As he proceeds to do this, he makes reference to his "honesty" and "courage." This is the significance of the book's title — *Honest to God*. These words, "honesty" and "courage," have strong emotional overtones and appeal to most people.

But is not this supposed courage rather the exact opposite, an unconsciously camouflaged attempt to please men? Out of fear of man, one seeks at all costs to make oneself understood, to adapt and adjust. And the fear of God, meanwhile, is lightly set aside. For the spiritual drift of our time is caused and characterized by this: This whole question of a "merciful God" has ceased to be a relevant question for modern man. It is now a "merciful brother" whom one seeks. More than ever, the words of Galatians 1:10 speak to us today: "Am I now seeking the favor of men, or of God? Or am I trying to please men? If I were still pleasing

[65] *Der Christliche Sonntag, Kath. Wochenblatt*, Herder, 3rd Sunday after Easter 1964

men, I should not be a servant of Christ." It was purportedly for the sake of "honesty" and "absolute candor" that the shameless film, *The Silence,* received support in Christian circles. We have already seen where such a false conception of honesty leads.

Does such "honesty" today actually require much courage? Hardly. The preparatory work has already been done by the atheistic giants like Nietzsche. The hearts of men have already been poisoned. They are open to any new teaching, such as this, which deposes God. The field is ripe for the proclamation of this modern theological teaching. At the outset one could have predicted a wide response to *Honest to God.* For the heart of man is already inclined to oppose God's absolute claims.

Today it is quite another kind of "honesty" which requires courage, real courage: This is the confession of faith in the God who lives, who made heaven and earth. Those who let the Biblical message stand as it is can expect little but disdain in many Christian and theological circles today. Today it costs something to testify that God is the Lord of life and history, the Judge of mankind, before whom every individual must appear for a final reckoning. One can count on being regarded as somewhat ridiculous among Christians today, if one speaks of God's holy wrath and coming judgment — to say nothing of citing some of the signs of such impending wrath, such as the threat of atomic war. Most people regard it as backward and old-fashioned to believe in a God who still works miracles today, who intervenes and helps. For many it is strange to trust a Father who loves us and hears our prayers. Stranger still that we are His children, redeemed by His only-begotten Son, who may love Him in return. The joy over such grace has faded away in much of Christianity.*

Today it takes courage to swim against the stream. The cry for a "revolution in ethics" is heard everywhere, and not least in Christian circles. It goes out to all lands, as if on ether waves. Those who dare to regard the old-fashioned Ten Commandments as God's absolute imperatives will not be taken seriously. But if the Church today is not to become powerless and spineless, she must swim against the stream. If she is to fulfill her mission, to be the salt of the earth, then she must summon up courage. She must be prepared to be a stumbling block, a "scandal," as was her Lord and Master.

This is also true in the ecumenical movement. Here also the danger of conforming to the spirit of the times lurks in the background. For today every fellowship is tempted to find God purely in the encounter between man and man. The temptation is to think that the only way you can experience God is through humanitarian fellowship, in the readiness to serve others, in fraternity. God, as the center of our lives, as the God who has once-for-all revealed himself, is more or less dispensed with. This striving to find God in the encounter between man and man becomes a self-perpetuating endeavor. One is driven to encounters and unions which are no longer "in Christ Jesus," but are grounded purely on human fellowship. This last danger is evident in certain aspects of the ecumenical movement today.

Certainly we can be thankful that the barriers between the different denominations are beginning to come down. (We must freely confess that these walls, built up over the centuries, were used mostly as vantage points for taking potshots at fellow Christians!) With these barriers removed, brethren in Christ can extend the hand of love to one another. They can thus give visible expression to the command of Jesus that His disciples should love one another. For by this sign alone will others recognize them as disciples of Jesus and come to believe in their Master. We all know what shame Christianity has brought upon the Name of Jesus with its internal strife and quarrels with one another. It has made Jesus incredible in the eyes of the non-Christian world.

Over and over again we have grieved Him by disregarding His last request. So we can be thankful whenever this last request of Jesus is taken seriously, and on the basis of it one seeks encounters with other denominations.

Yet for the ecumenical movement the danger remains: If we are not wide-awake, we will succumb to the temptation of being drawn into a falsely grounded humanitarian fellowship. This would lead to a false unity with all the world's religions. That would mean giving up Christ Himself. There are already disconcerting signs of such a movement. The remarks of a leading contemporary theologian, for instance, tend in just this direction. A treatise of his on the subject was termed by South German Radio as "undoubtedly one of the most significant events of modern intellectual history." In 1963 he spoke in Stuttgart on the theme: "The Absolute Claims of Christianity and the World Religions."

"The attempt to convert some of another faith" — which means merely to carry out the missionary command of Jesus — "is out of the question . . . when you want to convert another person, you are not taking him seriously."

But is not exactly the opposite the case? If a man is drowning, and I take his situation at all seriously, I must do nothing less than throw him a life-line. To "leave him alone" would not be to take him seriously, but to ignore his desperate plight.

It is a matter of course for Robinson, who relies heavily on such theology, to lead up to religion-in-general in his book. On this point the *Evangelische Kirchenzeitung* (Evangelical Church Newspaper) wrote: "Practical expediencies have led the way in the ecumenical movement. Theological considerations have lagged behind. Robinson's book offers a theological basis for many things already in practice. His initial assertion points the way: There is no separation between the Church and the world, between atheists and Christians; and the irreligious are also regarded as already under the sway of the Gospel of Christ. . . ."[66]

Real dangers beset the ecumenical movement: Instead of fulfilling Jesus' last request, it could lead to a blurring of distinctions. This could lead in time to a "Common Religion," which would pave the way for the Antichrist. He would take it and use it with deadly purpose. This Common Religion would not likely remain merely an idea. It would lead to a new existence for mankind. For this would give the Antichrist a spiritual basis for building his political empire, just as Marx did with his philosophical ideas.

In view of this, it becomes more important than ever that believers live out the "true ecumenical spirit," based on the love of our Lord Jesus Christ, and the claims of His commandments. This means that He must occupy the central position. This cannot be usurped by "human existence" or "concern for one's fellow man." Our love for Him surely allows us to embrace all that He Himself loved. But it also allows us to suffer with Him over all who do not love Him in return, and who disregard His commandments. True "ecumenical love" has always shown itself most clearly in suffering, for this reveals the one who is truly concerned for the Lord. Times of suffering and persecution are times of separation, as we experienced during the Nazi era. Then it becomes evident who is truly a disciple of Jesus. Such will always seek one another out in love. This will become more and more the case, the closer we approach the time of the Antichrist. Then all who love God and want to follow His commandments will suffer persecution as one.

All of this we must see clearly. We must consider the influences which are at work to confuse us. We must learn to strip away the pious mask from the many slogans which seem so convincing — "the spirit of humanity," "brotherly

---

[66]*Evang. Kirchenzeitung*, August 6, 1964

encounter," and so on. For our times are seriously threatened by a spirit of religious and moral deception. Our time, more than others before it, needs the glad message of the living God, the God who speaks: "Lo, I am here." Today, more than ever, we need the proclamation of the living God, who speaks and acts and takes a hand in our life, who hears our prayer and helps us. This is the word men are really waiting for, because mankind is sinking slowly into the quicksands of emptiness and despair.

Today we face a strange paradox: Many people have lost joy through an over-enjoyment of prosperity. To them we must proclaim the abundant joy to be found in the living Lord. The lack of satisfying personal relationships is characteristic of the world today. To this world we must proclaim the message of a God who loves men personally and intimately. God concerns Himself with every human being personally — we must do likewise. This does not mean "concern for one's fellow man," which cannot get beyond the boundary of our sinful human existence. It means a love which comes as a gift from the holy and living God, when we encounter Him.

One often hears it said today that mankind is in a "hopeless mess." That is the very reason that modern man needs the Gospel — the "good news" of the Saviour who has come bringing resurrection power for body, soul and spirit. He alone can help. And He is ready to step into our situation, whatever it may be, when we receive Him into our life as Lord.

Today man has fallen so deeply into sin that he needs to hear God's uncompromising judgment regarding sin and guilt. For only where sin is confessed and repented of does one experience the divine grace of forgiveness through the sacrifice of Jesus. And where that is experienced a shout of joy goes up! There men are redeemed and become new creatures in Christ.

Today the Church is doubly responsible to "live the Gospel" in everyday life. For it is through the living witness of the Church that this joyous Gospel of God's love seeks out the lost sinner. The Church will do this when she recognizes all her stiff, dead, pharisaic "faith"; when she is ready each day to present her wants and her failures before God and men, and confess, "God, be merciful to me, a sinner." This is how a true fellowship lives, in mutual forgiveness in Jesus Christ.

In such a fellowship the reality of God — the living God who reveals Himself — becomes evident. Where men believe in Him and honor Him as Lord, He makes Himself known. In His Church, and with the individual believer, He reveals Himself as the Creator of something new.

Jesus Christ forgives sin and makes one truly blessed. This should be evident in our lives. And this happens when one confesses his sin and guilt, when one hates the sin in his life and is determined to be free of it at any cost. This proves that sin, too, is a reality to us. And where one lives in joy because sin is forgiven, one also lives in the faith that Jesus makes all things new. This is a life of joy and comfort, rather than a life of despair, in the wastelands of nihilism. In this life Jesus proves Himself to be Saviour and Redeemer.

Today more than ever before, the life and the testimony of the Church must be "in Spirit and in truth." Only then will she be armed against theological influences which preach the Gospel with many of the old forms and expressions, but without explaining that something quite different is meant. Where the Church falls prey to this danger, she will begin more and more to revolve around "man." Many of the Biblical ideas may remain, but the living God, who reveals Himself, with His claim of love and holiness, will no longer be at the center. As this takes place, the Christian Church in many respects no longer lives with a Biblical orientation, but with a secular orientation — merely a citizen of one of the kingdoms of this world.

II.

IS THERE STILL HOPE?

The Reality of the Other Kingdom

"Repent, for the kingdom of heaven is at hand!" (Matthew 4:17). Like a Royal Proclamation, accompanied by the fanfare of trumpets, these words of Jesus sounded out over the world . . . a world which "is passing away" (I Corinthians 7:31). *His Kingdom* — this was the simple proclamation of Jesus. And in His own Person this "kingdom of heaven had come nigh."

Many have been baptized in His Name. Many may even call themselves His disciples. Yet few are really citizens of His Kingdom. Few there are who live in the world and yet, according to Jesus' word, "are not of the world" (John 17:14); who are hated by the world because they have been chosen out of the world (John 15:18, 19).

The true nature of the citizens of this Kingdom is revealed by the names they carry. The Lord of the Kingdom has Himself given the names: His *chosen* and *beloved* ones (Colossians 3:12). They have been summoned apart from the great mass of people whose thoughts revolve simply around their own human existence. For these, God alone is all-important. The citizens of the Kingdom of God are called "beloved" by their Lord. This is their surpassing joy.

Present-day Christianity, insofar as it has fallen victim to "modern" unbiblical thinking, has lost its contact with God. Not so with the citizens of His Kingdom. For these "beloved" of God, He is the great *Thou* of their lives. He is their whole love. He is their all in all — so much so, that even in the darkest hours of suffering, the Word lives in their hearts: "Whom have I in heaven but thee? And there is nothing upon earth that I desire besides thee. My flesh and my heart may fail, but God is the strength of my heart and my portion forever" (Psalm 73:25, 26). The "love of God" is the Alpha and Omega of their lives, the beginning and the end. Their relationship to God is no cool, intellectual affair: it is blood-warm. Their hearts beat with a love and a reverence for Jesus Christ, the King of this Kingdom, whose citizens they are privileged to be. In the Spirit, they come to Him in adoration. They bow low before Him. He is Lord. He is King. In His hand is goodness and blessing. His love is His wealth, and He spends it freely upon His beloved. His heart is ever open to forgive. They honor Him as a King and Lord who offered His life for His subjects, and so became also their Priest. He is a King of great power, yet He uses His power only to serve His subjects. In Him they have seen a King full of grace and glory. He reflects the very glory of God. He is a King of profound knowledge and wisdom, which He uses to guide those who have been entrusted to Him. He is a King who is love itself. Truly, His love streams through this Kingdom like the rising sun, for light is the child of love.

For the citizens of this Kingdom, who belong to Him, this is a Kingdom of happiness. Love makes it that. God's love brings happiness. The love in this Kingdom is many-sided. The One who sits upon the throne is not only the Ruler: He is also Father and Bridegroom. In former times He made a covenant of love with the citizens of His Kingdom — with God's people in the Old Testament — the marriage covenant at Sinai. Through the sacrificial death of Jesus, this love-covenant passed over into the New Testament. In the Kingdom of God, therefore, the relationship of the Ruler to His people is one of intimate love. And on the other hand, in the relationship of the people to their Lord, love is the decisive factor. Thus the Ruler has established only one law to govern the citizens of this Kingdom in their life together: *love one another*.

Love reigns as queen in the heavenly Kingdom. All love each other. Should not the Kingdom of God upon earth be a reflection of this heavenly Kingdom? For Jesus, who Himself is eternal love, came upon this earth and announced: "The Kingdom of God is in the midst of you" (Luke 17:21). In other words, a foreshadowing of the Kingdom of God has already broken in upon us, wherever Christ gains entrance, and His Lordship is established over our hearts and lives. At present this Kingdom, as a life-together-with-Christ, is "hidden in God" (Colossians 3:3). For upon earth this "mutuality of love" is still lived by sinners. Over and over they sin against love. Nevertheless, when they live according to Jesus' commandments, His citizens do portray something of the Kingdom of love. Despite the sins and failures, the kingly power of Jesus is made known. For His citizens have their eyes ever upon their Ruler. With His death upon the cross, He became the literal embodiment of forgiving love. Can His citizens do aught else but again and again forgive and be reconciled with one another? In this very act they portray love in its deepest sense.

This is the secret of citizens of the Kingdom. Their life together in Jesus Christ is characterized by mutual forgiveness and support. This becomes abundantly evident in a sisterhood or brotherhood, where one actually lives together with fellow Christians, to a greater or lesser degree. Each of us who has been a member of such a close-knit fellowship can testify to this. The great joy which one finds in such a life together roots in the continued renewal of forgiveness and concern among the members. One is continually challenged to forget himself and seek out his neighbor. In such repentance, the sacrifice of Jesus finds soil in which to grow. And His word becomes a reality: "The Kingdom of God is in your midst." This Kingdom of Jesus, this Kingdom of love, becomes the happy environment in which one lives his life. It is a foretaste of heaven, where joy will know no end.

Can our songs to this Lord ever end? Can we ever praise Him enough? The door of Paradise was closed. In Him it is thrown open again. He takes us into His Kingdom, the Kingdom of God. Once again He lives and reigns in the midst of His people. In His Kingdom, the deepest longings of men are stilled. Here one finds union with God, a gift from His fatherly hand. Here men may live with Him who made them, and loved them from eternity. This Kingdom of God "in the midst of us" foreshadows the Great Day which is drawing near: On that Day His Kingdom — the Kingdom of love, peace, joy, and light — will become visible to all the world, and will endure forever.

The one truth which becomes clear in the Kingdom is this: Real love between people is born only out of a true love and reverence toward God. Here one knows nothing of "concern for one's fellow man" which is not dependent upon the First Commandment: "You shall love the Lord your God with all your heart, and with all your soul, and with all your mind" (Matthew 22:37). Here one knows nothing of a false "compassion," which counts it a virtue to look with indulgence upon the sins of a neighbor. A disregard for God's commandments, which separates the sinner from God, cannot be salved away with the slogan of "compassion."

Love toward man, which is firmly fixed on God, leaves no emptiness in its wake. Love rooted in God is full of eternal divine life. It endures forever. The very nature of this love, which is rooted in God, is to do good to others. This love is true. It is kind — amiable — sympathetic. It makes others happy — and finds therein its own happiness! This love is a ray of the divine love with which God loves us. And therefore the power which it bears within itself is opposite in nature from the power of human love which has separated itself from God. Its motive is not to "live life to the full and be happy." Its motive is to give oneself without reservation to God and one's neighbor. It is a priestly love which does not shrink from sacrifice. It makes others rich. Instead of emptiness, it brings forth joy and fruit.

Love which bears the stamp of nihilism is "love without hope." By contrast this divine love brings with it the precious treasure of hope. And therefore it is a waiting and expectant love. In His Kingdom, the beloved of God live in hope. They await the coming of Him whom they love — Jesus, their Lord, Redeemer, and Bridegroom. The King of their realm let it be known, as He ascended into heaven, that He would come again in like manner as He had gone. He clearly prophesied His coming again. Indeed, He spoke of a day on which He would come to His chosen ones and with them establish His Kingdom (Matthew 24:31). Those who love Jesus have their sights set upon this coming Kingdom.

In other words, they are not merely concerned about their own personal salvation. They have a concern, together with their Lord, for the Kingdom of God itself. For them it is not enough simply to say: "I believe in Jesus, I am baptized, I am converted, I am born again." The Bible knows nothing of a lone-wolf Christianity. The disciple of Jesus knows that God's Word — above all, knows that Jesus Himself — emphasized one thing above all others: The Kingdom of God. This was Jesus' message as He began His public ministry. Again, this was the great theme of the conversations He held with His disciples during the forty days following His resurrection: The Kingdom of God (Acts 1:3). And through His Apostle John, in the last book of the Bible, He let the message of the coming Kingdom be renewed once again. At the end of time, Jesus will no longer permit His Kingdom to shine as a mere token in the darkness of the world. Rather, the kingdoms of this world will then stand visible and exposed under His Lordship.

The message of the Kingdom of God therefore involves not only the individual, nor only the Church of Jesus Christ in the world, but it involves all the nations of the world. For this is the cry that peals through heaven in the end times, when the judgments are poured out on the earth: "The kingdom of the world has become the kingdom of our Lord and of his Christ" (Revelation 11:15). God loves the world: It shall be renewed. This is the concern of God and the central theme of the joyous message of the Bible.

The disciples of Jesus look forward to the coming Kingdom. Their expectations are altogether different from other people. The disciples of Jesus believe neither in the progressive development of mankind, nor in the destruction of mankind in a final judgment. They believe in the coming Kingdom, because Jesus is the Lord and King who is coming again. Before them is a great and glorious goal. The world shall be changed and set free and renewed. For this they live. For this they prepare themselves.

Oh, they see clearly the approaching judgments of God. They are not blind to the signs of the times. But they see beyond: They know that the judgments of God which are coming upon the nations are only an intermediate stage. They represent only a short stretch of man's history, though a very dark one. Then Jesus will come again. He will bring the new heaven and the new earth in which righteousness shall dwell (II Peter 3:13). So they know that their waiting will end in joy, joy unspeakable. Therefore, when the terrible judgments of God begin, they lift up their heads, for they know that redemption draws nigh — not only for them personally, but for mankind, for the perishing earth (Luke 21:28). And so, in the dark midnight hour, they call to one another, *"Maranatha,* our Lord comes!" Yes, already they sing with great joy the hymn of glory at the ascendancy of the

King of kings: "The kingdoms of this world have become the kingdom of our Lord and of his Christ, and he shall reign for ever and ever" (Revelation 11:15). So they sing, together with the Church Triumphant, even as the judgments of God are poised over the earth.

Those who are His live in keen anticipation of Jesus' return, and of the Kingdom of God which shall come in glory. His love has planted this hope in their hearts. And therefore they are delivered from the senseless, dismal life of our times, with its hopelessness and nihilism. They know that God's history is moving toward a positive goal, an end. This guards them against the great danger of being left out of history, which so threatens Christianity in our day. Men no longer believe in *Heilsgeschichte,* "salvation history," in which God in all His ways moves toward a clearly defined goal, which is the coming and establishment of His Kingdom.

Yet nothing less than this "hour of salvation," the final goal of history, will bring redemption to the world. Those who belong to Him cry for this redemption. They suffer for mankind which threatens to go under in the quicksands of godlessness and immorality. They are not blind. They see the rank growth and corruption of sin. They see how rottenness and the dissolution of all order is spreading to all fields. And therefore they pray and plead to God for the grace of repentance. Year after year, with increasing intensity, they call upon men to turn and repent before the "great and terrible day of the Lord" comes. For many can yet be rescued from destruction.

Yet at the same time there comes from their hearts the irrepressible cry: "The King is coming. Prepare yourselves for the day of His glory!" Year by year this call swells and grows in the company of believers, until it becomes a mighty demonstration before the hosts of heaven, "Come soon, Lord Jesus!" It is the outcry of those who see that mankind, in wild rebellion against Him and His commandments, have made His earth a hell of destruction. Therefore those who belong to Him cry out: Lord, establish Thy Kingdom, that the earth be not consigned to hell forever! It is the cry of the bridal company, who watch with deep longing for the coming of the King and Bridegroom.

The entire life of the citizens of the Kingdom of God, in these end times, is full of such calls and cries to God. For they heed Jesus' words concerning the signs of the times. With the spiritual intuition of those who love God, they sense that the Kingdom of God is at the very door. Yes, the hour is near when "the kingdom and the dominion and the greatness of the kingdoms under the whole heaven shall be given to the people of the saints of the Most High; their kingdom shall be an everlasting kingdom, and all dominions shall serve and obey them" (Daniel 7:27).

And their joy over this is no delusion and intoxication of the senses. It is not a reverie which, when it is past, will drop them back into a cold, empty reality. For the Kingdom of God is more true and real than the kingdoms of the world. This is so even now, when it but foreshadows the future glory. The final and deepest reality is that which does not fade away, but which abides.

A horrible awakening, however, will follow the power delirium of man today. Taking a bold Nietzschian posture, he calls out: "Our rockets have passed the moon. We did not discover God. We have extinguished the lights of heaven!" The awakening will come when the judgment of God descends, and men, earth, and planets are destroyed in a moment. Man today lives for greater and greater displays of human power. But already, behind it, there is a specter of helplessness and despair. For what good will it do man even to pass the moon, if God lets earth and moon be consumed in fire?

But the citizens of the Kingdom of God live in true safety in time and in eternity. They have solid ground under their feet. They stand on the Rock of Jesus Christ and His Word. What a privilege — to live with Jesus hour by hour! He is ever at their side. They can talk with Him. He guides and helps them — He to whom all power has been given in heaven and on earth. When the terrors of atomic war come — the frightful judgment of God's wrath — they know themselves protected in the shelter of His love. They have already experienced in their lives that God remains faithful to His Word: "God is faithful, and he will not let you be tempted (tested) beyond your strength, but with the temptation (testing) will also provide the way of escape, that you may be able to endure it" (I Corinthians 10:13).

His people are sure of this: According to His Word, God will act on behalf of His own in the dark days that are coming. In the hour of great distress He will prove the truth of His Name, "Jehovah — I am." He will remain true to His Word, "Lo, I am with you always" (Matthew 28:20). When Jesus is with us, He turns the storm to calm, fear to comfort. Yes, He will also do signs and wonders according to His Word: "Our God is a God of salvation" (Psalm 68:20), and: "Thou art the God who workest wonders" (Psalm 77:14). He will give even miraculous protection and help, in ways appropriate to His love and power. His people dare believe this. He is a Ruler, but He is also the Good Shepherd. He tends His sheep with great love, leads them to green pastures and also through dark valleys. In these dark times, God's people will be privileged to experience a safekeeping in Him. And this will itself be a foreshadowing of God's glorious Kingdom.

But who may enter this Kingdom? Who will be received as a citizen? Jesus said: "Enter by the narrow gate" (Matthew 7:13). Above this gate one word is written, which forces a decision upon all who would enter: "*Repent. The Kingdom of God is at hand.*" The gate to the New Jerusalem allows no unauthorized person to enter (Revelation

21:27). Likewise the gate to this unique Kingdom allows no one to enter who opposes the authority of the Lord of the Kingdom. This gate has the power to turn back those whose faith is dead, who therefore have no fruit of the Spirit. If a man tries to enter before he has come to true repentance through the power of Jesus' blood the gate closes in his face.

At this gate every person encounters a call that goes out like the voice of a trumpet: 'Turn about! Repent! To the mighty, humble yourself — to him who has lived in contention with men, be reconciled — to him who has held on to his own possessions, give them up — to him who in sin has followed his own desires, turn back from sinful ways" (Ephesians 4:22). Every relationship to another person which cannot be justified before God must be broken off. This includes relationships to the opposite sex which God would look upon as adultery according to the Sermon on the Mount (see also I Corinthians 6:9-10). And to him who judges others and is angry, who speaks ill of others — put away evil talk, for "those who do such things shall not inherit the Kingdom of God" (Galatians 5:19-21). Neither here nor above will such ones have any part in the Kingdom of God. They will belong to the realm which corresponds to their dark lives, the kingdom of darkness and torment of which we can get a taste even here on earth.

What a difference between the gate to God's Kingdom and the gate into the kingdom of this world. The kingdom of this world is characterized by lust for power. The inscription over its gate reads: "Be prepared to make good your claims against God and man." It means making your own way in the midst of revolt, rebellion and hate. The man who stands before this gate has broken away from God. In his mind he has fashioned a kingdom based on his own wishes. He believes the kingdom of this earth will fulfill his dreams. As he strides through the gate, he lifts his head high — asserting confidence in himself and thereby in his sin.

But he who truly encounters the living God and desires to enter His Kingdom, humbles himself in reverence. He comes before a great Lord and Ruler, who made heaven and earth, who is holy and almighty. He comes before his holy Creator and Judge, knowing full well that he himself is a sinner. Of himself, he cannot stand in His presence. Of himself, he cannot be a citizen of His Kingdom. Yet in daily repentance for all that is against the royal commandments of this Lord and King, the gate of the Kingdom swings open. In the power of Jesus' sacrifice, as one "holy and beloved," he will go the way of God's commandments.

Laws of the Kingdom — an Unchanging Offer of Divine Love

JESUS IMPRESSED THIS WORD upon His disciples: "If you love me, you will keep my commandments" (John 14:15; also John 14:21, 23). And the Apostle John witnesses to the same great truth: "This is the love of God, that we keep his commandments" (I John 5:3). Do we believe in Jesus as the Lord of His Kingdom? Do we love Him? This faith and this love is confirmed and lived out as we accept the laws of His Kingdom. This is what characterizes those who are true citizens of the Kingdom of God.

All commandments in the Kingdom of God are summarized in the two chief commandments which Jesus gave in answer to the question of the Sadducees: No other commandment is greater than these two, "You shall love the Lord your God with all your heart, and with all your soul, and with all your mind. This is the great and first commandment. And a second is like it, You shall love your neighbor as yourself" (Mark 12:31; Matthew 22:37-39). These twin laws of love cannot be separated from each other: "By this we know that we love the children of God, when we love God and obey his commandments" (I John 5:2); and "He who loves God should love his brother also" (I John 4:21). This commandment of love is the "old commandment which you had from the beginning" (I John 2:7) — in other words, in the Old Testament. That is why Jesus answered the Sadducees with this old commandment from Sinai. On the other hand, Jesus' beloved disciple John writes, "Yet I am writing you a new commandment" (I John 2:8). He means this in the sense of Jesus' words: "A new commandment I give you, that you love one another; even as I have loved you, that you also love one another" (John 13:34).

When God made the covenant of the Old Testament with His people at Sinai, the essential content of His commandments was love toward God and love toward man. He gave these commandments in order to establish "a kingdom of priests and a holy nation" (Exodus 19:6). This kingdom was to be a kingdom of love. As a priestly people, their one concern should be to love God. Him they would serve continually, in worship, devotion and sacrifice. This priestly people should be His own possession among all peoples, for all the earth is His (Exodus 19:5). This people, then, should minister to all men, in priestly and sacrificial love. They should be a bridge between men and God.

The laws of the Kingdom, then, were based upon love from the beginning. The objective of the laws was determined by the nature of God Himself, which is love. These laws would characterize this "kingdom of priests," and give it its peculiar stamp. On Sinai, God made His will known in the Ten Commandments. The people did not hear frightening commands come forth from His mouth, such as other peoples supposedly heard from the mouths of their gods. That is something to inspire awe and worship. Yet how could it be otherwise, than that God's laws would be laws of love! For they are not given by a king to his subjects, but from a God "who is your husband" (Isaiah 54:5). God's commandments were given as the basis for a *marriage*! Israel was God's partner — He calls her His wife (Isaiah 54:6; 62:4). These "commandments for marriage," therefore, were the most precious treasure of His heart. With these commandments He truly opened His heart to Israel. In His Son, our Lord Jesus Christ, He offers them also to us. Is it not the greatest offer and gift one could imagine?

The citizens of the Kingdom of God know that they are loved by God, the Ruler of the Kingdom. They are privileged to love God, because God permits it, indeed He invites it. The first commandment actually implies this happy thought: You shall — you *may* — love Me with all your heart, life, spirit, mind, soul, and strength — your entire being. You may love Me with all your abilities, with every breath. In this love, God gives Himself freely to us. And this suggests the practical measure of love which He expects in return: Give Me your whole heart, your whole life, the best part of your time, your money, all that you have, all that you hold dear, be it people or things. Give it to Me. Let Me have charge of it. Then you will know the truth of the word, "All that is mine is yours" (Luke 15:31).

With such commands "to love," God gives His children a foretaste of Paradise. Who is more to be loved and desired than the Father of our Lord Jesus Christ? Or the Lord, Saviour, and Redeemer Himself? To love such a God is itself the essence of Paradise (see John 17:3). Indeed, this Kingdom of God bears the character of Paradise. One could rightly term the laws of His Kingdom "Paradise laws." For something of Paradise breaks in wherever men live according to these laws. The sunlight of God — the sunlight of joy — streams upon those who go the way of His commandments, in the footsteps of Jesus.

What a Ruler we have! What wisdom and glory in His commandments! Can His citizens in this kingdom of priests do aught else but break forth in praise and adoration? Indeed, we can never praise enough the King of this realm. We must join the Psalmist in his praise of God's commandments: "My lips shall pour forth Thy praise for Thou dost teach me Thy statutes." The commandments of God are the most precious revelation of His love, a window into His innermost heart. They are His sweetest gift to the sons of men, the delight of their hearts, light on the pathway, words of counsel from Him. How dearly they are to be prized! His commandments are pure truth. They bring the fullness of salvation, and peace like a river. True citizens of His Kingdom rejoice over the commandments of God, "as one who takes great spoil." The commandments of God are more precious to His people than gold and silver. They are the wondrous outpouring of His thoughts — "how precious to me are Thy Thoughts." They alone are altogether right. They are holy and wonderful (see Psalm 139). Jesus often sang praises to the commandments, as He sang the Psalms with His disciples. Surely they knew well Psalm 119, which is so full of praise for God's commandments. The early Church continued this manner of praise from the Psalms (Ephesians 5:19; Colossians 3:16).

Words simply fail to praise the perfection of the commandments which God gave for His Kingdom. How imperfect, by comparison, are the laws of many countries today. Often they lead to distress and even death. If the rulers are filled with hatred toward God or toward a particular group of people, such as another race, their laws will have the same hateful character. When we see such laws in operation, we should all the more give glory to our Lord for His wonderful commandments.

Today all the commandments and ordinances of God are crumbling away. His laws are abolished and made the object of mockery. The rebellion against His commandments has penetrated right into His Church. The Lord calls us to take a stand against all of this and let it be clearly known that for us these laws are holy and beloved. In no other way can we build a dam against the flood of lawlessness.

Our day desperately needs to hear the glad testimony: "Thy statutes have been my songs in the house of my pilgrimage . . . Thy testimonies are my delight, they are my counselors. . . . How sweet are thy words to my taste, sweeter than honey to my mouth. . . . My soul keeps thy testimonies; I love them exceedingly. . . . Oh, how I love thy law! It is my meditation all the day" (all from Psalm 119). Truly such commandments are to be praised! Commandments given to us out of the heart of God's love, out of the depths of His wisdom and understanding! In praising the commandments, we praise God Himself, who gave them.

The wonder of God's law is only seen by those who actually "run in the way of his commandments" (verse 32). From them, the real citizens of the Kingdom of God, will be heard the songs of praise for these commandments of love. For in all ages they bring to those who keep them, blessing, salvation, joy, peace, the rich gifts of heaven — yes, for time and eternity. Who can but rejoice over such things? It is the haughty and self-righteous who do not rejoice. We see that in history. It is always the proud, self-confident ones who set up their own laws. But in so doing — consciously or unconsciously — they despise and actually oppose the laws of God. In this one sees the proof of the truth which the Psalmist records: "Before I was afflicted (humbled), I went astray, but now I keep thy word" (verse 67).

Not everyone breaks through to this joy and love for God's commandments. It is for the humble. It is for the true subjects of the realm, who submit to the Lord's rule. To the others the commandments seem hard demands. The "proudly exultant" ones (the Bible's term at one time for a certain superficial "piety") also find no joy in them (Zephaniah 3:11). All of these are not able to join in praising the commandments.

But do not many of the commandments indeed contain "hard demands"? Are all of them really linked to the basic commandment of love: "You shall love the Lord your God above all things, and your neighbor as yourself"? It is true that we find a whole list of commandments in the Old Testament, besides the Ten Commandments. Many of these had to do with Israel's outward situation at that time. And yet they are all fashioned by the same Spirit of love. We might picture the twin commandment of love, the Ten Commandments, and the many other commandments as a tree with many branches. The root of the tree is the twin commandment of love which Jesus gave — love God and neighbor. All other commandments grow out of this. The Ten Commandments form the trunk of the tree. Further commandments are represented by the many limbs and branches. A great many of these were given just for the geographical, political, or cultural situation of Israel at that time. As circumstances changed, they ceased to have any meaning.

This would be true, for instance, of the commandment: "If you ever take your neighbor's garment in pledge, you shall restore it to him before the sun goes down; for that is his only covering, it is his mantle for his body; in what else shall he sleep? And if he cries to me, I will hear, for I am compassionate" (Exodus 22:26-27). As soon as Israel no longer lived in the Orient, where a man's cloak was his only covering, this commandment ceased to have meaning. Yet there remains in this commandment the eternally valid principle: love is aware of the basic needs of the neighbor. The spiritual intent of this commandment may therefore apply today, in a figurative sense.

The laws concerning the priesthood and sacrifice must be interpreted in a different way. These laws were fulfilled in Jesus, our great High Priest who gave His own life as a living sacrifice for sin and guilt. By that act He verified that

He is the fulfillment of the Law. From that point on there is a change in the sacrifices which God's People bring to their God. "You are a holy priesthood, to offer spiritual sacrifices acceptable to God through Jesus Christ" (I Peter 2:5), writes the Apostle Peter to the Church. Now the Church of Jesus Christ brings spiritual sacrifices, since the many animal sacrifices have been superseded in the one perfect sacrifice of the Lamb of God. This happens as Jesus, the Head, draws His members into His life, His love, His sacrifice. For the New Testament Church has its roots in Calvary, where Jesus fulfilled the commandment of love. Now the Church fulfills the commandments. She brings spiritual sacrifices, as an act of love. She lives the commandments — in Jesus, and by the power of His Spirit.

Jesus became the fulfillment of God's commandments. He lived out the love which God's law demanded. In the Son of God, the commandment to love became flesh. The communication of God's commandments by word became a communication by incarnation. And so in the New Testament something mighty and great and altogether new takes place. In the Passion of Jesus, the tablets of the Law became a living demonstration. For He lived in complete harmony with the commandments. He truly loved God above all things, and His neighbor, His brother, as Himself (Hebrews 2:11; Romans 8:29). In this sense also Christ is the end of the Law, for in Him the Law took on living form. All that was written in the Law became an event and a reality in Jesus. Now the One and Only has come who could say, "I delight to do thy will, O my God; Thy law is within my heart" (Psalm 40:8). "Lo, I have come to do thy will" (Hebrews 10:7). And, "I know him and I keep his word" (John 8:55).

Keeping the commandments is therefore identical to following Jesus. This is the altogether new thing in our relationship to the commandments in the New Testament.

It has to do with Jesus Himself. To the extent that we seek by faith to live God's commandments of love, we offer praise to Him who embodies these commandments.

Jesus Christ Himself is thus the foundation upon which the pillars of God's Kingdom Laws stand. And therefore the edifice of this Kingdom is full of glory, for the foundation is the sacrificial love of God's Lamb, the incarnation of the commandments of love. The citizens of His Kingdom are now all those who, as stones, have been set into this foundation, who live the commandments of love as He does. And because this foundation is a living foundation, He calls to us: Come, follow Me! "For by this all men will know that you are my disciples, if you have love for one another" (John 13:35).

The one who wants to fulfill God's commandments of love does not have only outward instruction: He has a living example in whose path he may follow. It is the way of love, which laid down its own life, with all its claims and rights. "Who for the joy that was set before him endured the cross" (Hebrews 12:2). It is the way of love, which became poor, that others might become rich. It was a love which did not answer abuse with abuse, but rather endured patiently from sinners and enemies such injustice and hostility against Himself (Hebrews 12:3). It was a love which forgave those who did great evil against Him, and gave Him over to a death of torment, though He had done them only good. It was and is a love which suffers all that another might do to Him. It endures patiently, it blesses, it continues to love, in order that the other might amend. It is a love which comes to rule others through gentleness, and so establishes and governs the Kingdom.

This love, and no other, is the law of the realm in the Kingdom of Jesus Christ. Jesus has traveled the way ahead of us. His specific commands for everyday life are plain and simple directives. Their meaning cannot be changed to signify a general concept of "love." Jesus' directives are simple because all they do is to call us to follow in His footsteps. He has gone this way Himself, and therefore the way already has a specific mark and character. The way is marked by such acts as these: forgive and be reconciled with those who have done us wrong; go the second mile; give to him who asks; do good to our enemy, love him and bless him; invite those who are not our friends, whose ways are not pleasing to us.

Thus in the hearts of His disciples sounds the challenge and the promise: Love your enemy as your friend, and you will be God's friend; forgive from your heart him who does you injustice; for blessed are those who forgive; they will be forgiven by God. Take care that you make no charge and keep no tally in your heart of the evil done against you; forgive, and the greatest of all things will come to you, the forgiveness of your sins. Invite those who are repulsive to you, and you will be near to God. Do good to those who hate you, and God will overwhelm you with love. With your gifts, do not forget those who forget and overlook you; you will be a true child of your Father who also causes His sun to shine on the unrighteous. All of this is summed up in the words of Jesus: "Love your enemies . . . so that you may be sons of your Father who is in heaven" (Matthew 5:44, 45).

Time and again the Apostle John heard with his own ears these commandments out of the mouth of Jesus. And what does he say concerning these commandments of love? "His commandments are not burdensome" (I John 5:3). Why? Jesus, the Fulfiller of the commandments, lived them out to the death for us. He sacrificed His life for us. He loosed us from the chains of selfishness and lovelessness. He thus made it possible for us to keep the commandment of love. Of course, this takes place through a process of growth. We fail often, and stand again in need of forgiveness. Nevertheless, "I live; yet not I, but Christ lives in me" (Galatians

2:20). Wherever we give Him room, Jesus lives more and more in us. He fulfills His commandment of love in us through His Holy Spirit. What overflowing grace: The commandments and instructions of God have become a gift!

GOD'S COMMANDMENTS — STILL BINDING TODAY? RELEVANT OR OUTMODED?

AS THE CONTENT of the commandments is love, their nature is holiness and absoluteness, for they come from the mouth of the thrice-holy God. They are of supreme greatness and glory. God is eternal, all-wise, almighty. His commandments bear the stamp of His own absolute supremacy. They are eternally valid.

The rulers of this world give expression to their will in the laws they proclaim. These will come and go. High above these rulers of earth stands the eternal God. His commandments, like Himself, stand firm and will never change. Exalted and great is the Ruler and Lawgiver: Mighty are His commandments.

Mt. Sinai quaked as God gave His commandments, a unique testimony to the holiness of God and His commandments. All nature was astir — thunder and lightning — as God revealed Himself. Similarly at the death of Jesus the earth shook and the rocks were split, and the sun's light failed. At Sinai the Covenant of the Law was sealed with blood (Exodus 24:8). On Calvary Jesus sealed the New Covenant with His blood (Hebrews 9:26, 14). This parallel indicates that the sacrifice of Jesus, as a prophetic seed, lay hidden in the event at Sinai (Luke 24:27; John 5:39). And so the commandments stand today as they stood then, like Sinai itself, solid, immovable, granite. They are always valid, as the Psalmist says: "Every one of thy righteous ordinances endures forever" (Psalm 119:160).

Surely it lies within my power not to regard God's commandments as absolute. I can order my life by other commandments, which I give myself or allow others to give me. But in the end I cannot escape the claim of God, which He makes known in His commandments. The challenge of His commandments follows me into eternity itself. There, after my death, I will be judged according to those commandments. They will determine my destiny for all eternity. Therefore everything depends upon whether I regard and keep God's commandments or not. If I do not keep them, in a figure, Sinai will fall upon me and crush me. For Jesus, though He is our Lord and Saviour, speaks in the Sermon on the Mount of those who say "Lord, Lord," but do not live according to His will and His commandments. He calls them "evildoers" (Matthew 7:23). Jesus compares those who transgress the commandments of God to a man who builds his house on sand. He will come down with a crash when the floods come — the time of tribulation and judgment of God (Matthew 7:27).

When Jesus speaks such a word of judgment upon "evildoers," it should help us recognize how closely bound together are the Old Testament and the New Testament. It should show us that it is not "living in the Old Testament," in a false sense, when we bind ourselves to the commandments. Of course we recognize the exceptions, which obviously apply to Israel's special circumstances, and therefore are understood today in a figurative or analogical sense. But the commandments of Sinai, as such, are God's commandments, and therefore they are also Jesus' commandments. That is why Jesus lived out Sinai's commandments of love until it cost Him His life. The God of the Old Testament is the God of the New Testament, who has appeared in Jesus Christ. And conversely, Christ was also present in the Old Testament (I Corinthians 10:4).

Men today need to see the essential nature of the commandments. Indeed, we cannot make clear enough the absoluteness and the validity of the commandments for the

New Testament Church. "For ever, O Lord, thy word is firmly fixed in the heavens" (Psalm 119:89). The commandments come out of God's heart, and all that comes out of God has eternal significance. It has validity for the aeons of man's history. God's commandments are the expression of His will. But behind the will are His thoughts. And here one encounters the wisdom of God — a depth and a breadth whose final significance man will never fully grasp. They are words in which a profound depth of love lies hidden. This love is so strong and ardent, so all-encompassing, that it gathers together in itself all human love — and yet that human love, compared to God's love, is like a drop in an ocean.

Thus the commandments stand before us, unchanged and unchangeable. They call us to decision whether we will or no. "You shall not bear false witness against your neighbor." Whoever transgresses this commandment is guilty over against God and man. He has made disparaging remarks about his neighbor. Without checking the facts, he has spread untrue statements which damage the neighbor's honor and reputation. Where this guilt is not confessed before God and man, and no forgiveness obtained, it remains. Before God's Judgment Throne such a one will one day be judged according to the Eighth Commandment and found guilty. If he protests, "But I believed in Jesus!" — he will receive the reply, "In Christ avails only the faith which works through love" (Galatians 5:6). Love makes no disparaging remarks about another, to say nothing of outright injustice or malice.

The Sixth Commandment is also eternally valid: "Thou shall not commit adultery." Some people say that God's commandments are no longer binding, because they belong to the Old Testament. At the point of this commandment they will see how false their conception is. In the Sermon on the Mount Jesus brings a far broader obligation to bear regarding this commandment. His demands make one shudder: Adultery is committed when one so much as looks upon the opposite sex with lust. "If your right eye causes you to sin, pluck it out and throw it away; it is better that you lose one of your members than that your whole body be thrown into hell" (Matthew 5:29).

In regard to the Fifth Commandment, one sees again the intensity of Jesus' demands: One is likened to a murderer when he but speaks abusive, angry words to another. The other may well have irritated us, but Jesus' judgment stands: "Whoever says to his brother, 'You fool!' shall be liable to the hell of fire" (Matthew 5:22).

Thus Jesus lays out standards more absolute in character than what one saw in the commandments of the Old Testament. In the Old Testament the words of the Lord were like a knife to the marrow: After He had given the commandments, He said that Israel's very life would depend upon whether she kept them or not. And He drove this word into their conscience: "I call heaven and earth to witness against you this day, that I have set before you life and death, blessing and curse" (Deuteronomy 30:19). Now Jesus has deepened the understanding of God's commandments, as commandments of love. He has laid them on our hearts with great urgency. And therefore He speaks an even more dreadful judgment over those who do not keep these commandments of love. Love demands the most because it gives the most. To sin against love, therefore, incurs the greatest guilt.

Moses prophesied, "The Lord will raise up for you a prophet like me from among you — him shall you heed" (Deuteronomy 18:15). Jesus is that second Moses. He takes up the Old Testament commandments and makes them His own. For there are those who term them "for Old Testament times," in a negative sense. They hold them as no longer binding for the New Testament Church. From such Jesus protects the commandments, down to our own day. He underscores and strengthens God's law. He takes His stand with the Old Testament Law because it expresses the commands of God's loving will. He portrays the individual commandments in terms of their deepest sense and content, tracing them back to the primeval will of God, which is love. "Not a jot or tittle," Jesus says, "will pass from the law" (Matthew 5:18). And He points out what He means by this, namely, the spiritual content of these commandments.

The Law is a testimony of the divine will. It expresses an eternally valid moral and religious truth. In no way is it repealed or set aside in the New Testament. By bringing the Old Testament commandments into the Sermon on the Mount for special attention, Jesus indicated that they were to have eternal validity. The Law is given to the Christian as a guideline for all times. In the last dreadful judgments which come upon the earth, the elements will melt in heat, and heaven and earth will pass away. But the commandments of God will not pass away. They will remain and retain their validity precisely in our time, when the first shadows of the Antichrist Kingdom begin to lengthen upon the earth.

In these last days, the Church must be more watchful of the commandments than anything else. In Luther's time the false idea of justification by works had the upper hand. The need of that day was to bring justification by faith to light. Today the Church lives to a great extent on "cheap grace." Mankind as a whole is gripped by the spirit of lawlessness. The Church must pay heed to the message of the Bible for the last days. In the *Revelation* to John we read, "Here is a call for the endurance of the saints, those who keep the commandments of God and the faith of Jesus" (Revelation 14:12).

The Apostle Peter also writes for the last days in his second epistle. He portrays a time like our own, describing men who "indulge in the lust of defiling passion and despise authority . . . they are like irrational animals, creatures of instinct, born to be caught and killed . . . they have eyes full of adultery, insatiable for sin . . . uttering loud boasts of folly, they entice with licentious passions of the flesh men who have barely escaped from those who live in error" (II Peter 2:10, 12, 14, 18). Why have men fallen into such lives of sin? Because "they have turned back from the holy commandment delivered to them" (verse 21). Indeed, the Apostle Peter says here: "It would have been better for them never to have known the way of righteousness than after knowing it to turn back from God's commandments" (verse 21). That is how decisive he considers this fact of whether the believers keep the commandments or not. It carries dreadful consequences. He speaks with unmistakable clarity of the judgment, darkness and punishment which awaits those who have lived in the sins of the flesh (verses 9, 17) — who are transgressors of the commandments.

Never before in the history of mankind has this one theme been so urgent: "The Ten Commandments, the Foundation of All Order." All around us are signs of chaos and demoralization. For we have not regarded these commandments. We have not lived by them. This summons up the Day of Judgment, in which the world and all the works of man will go up in flames. That will bring destruction upon man, as the Apostle Peter says (II Peter 3:10). The Church of Jesus Christ knows this. Therefore she has a priestly responsibility to remain watchful when the Sinai commandments, and thereby the foundations of the Bible, are being shaken.

REBELLION AGAINST GOD'S COMMANDMENTS — WHY?

IN THESE LAST DAYS, as never before, the People of God must take its stand upon the foundation of God's commandments. These are days when His Church must re-learn reverence, and stand in godly fear before the holy Lawgiver, the living God. False teaching is abroad in these last days.

It leads many astray, for it comes dressed in the old Biblical words and phrases, but the inner content of faith is changed. The Church must know where she stands, or she will fall prey to these new teachings. What is the distinctive mark which shows whether a teaching is from God or not? The disciple who was closest to Jesus once answered this question. His answer is still valid today: "Every spirit which confesses that Jesus Christ has come in the flesh is of God, and every spirit which does not confess Jesus is not of God. This is the spirit of antichrist" (I John 4:2-3).

If this confession is not central to the message, it is time to sound the alarm. It signifies that the enemy has already moved into battle position. Imperceptibly he sponges out of the creed faith in the Son-of-God-come-in-the-flesh, and love toward Him. At the same time he lets other ethical standards be proclaimed, which make the Ten Commandments relative, or indeed unnecessary. He attempts to strip God's commandments of their eternal and absolute claims, in the eyes of believers. He comes in scholar's garb: "God's commandments were for the Old Testament. They are not valid for the Church of the New Testament." But God's Word says: "He who says, 'I know him' but disobeys his commandments is a liar" (I John 2:4). Indeed, the Apostle John calls such ones "children of the devil" (I John 3:10). We must come to recognize Satan's technique of deception. Way back in the Garden of Eden he was saying, "Did God say . . .?" In like manner he wants to call into question the significance of the commandments in the setting of the New Testament.

These machinations are aimed against Jesus Himself. We recall His encounter with the Rich Young Ruler. "What shall I do," the man asked, "to have eternal life?" Jesus answered him, "If you would enter life, keep the commandments" (Matthew 19:17). Jesus' contention with those who were piously zealous about keeping the Law was precisely this, that they were not doing what God's Law demanded

(Matthew 23:23). Because they did not truly keep the Law, which was Jesus' chief concern, He said to the Pharisees: "Within you are full of hypocrisy and iniquity" (Matthew 23:28). "Depart from me you evildoers" (Matthew 7:23). Therefore He solemnly warns: "Whoever then relaxes one of the least of these commandments and teaches men so, shall be called least in the kingdom of heaven" (Matthew 5:19).

Paul also had concern for this, and asks rhetorically: "Do we then overthrow the law by this faith? By no means! On the contrary, we uphold the law" (Romans 3:31). For Paul, the Law was holy, just and good (Romans 7:12 and 14). He said of himself that he was not without law toward God, but rather was under the law of Christ (I Corinthians 9:21). He repeatedly points to the Law as a binding ordinance — for instance, "You shall not muzzle the ox when it is treading the grain" (Deuteronomy 25:4; I Corinthians 9:9; I Timothy 5:18). He says that it is hostility against God not to submit to His Law (Romans 8:7). It is evident that after his conversion, Paul still considered the Law holy and binding.

Paul, however, also appears to have a zeal for opposing the Law, and seems to contradict the statements mentioned above. He writes: "Now we are discharged (free) from the law" (Romans 7:6). In another place: "The law is not laid down for the just" (I Timothy 1:9). "He has broken down the dividing wall of hostility, by abolishing in his flesh the law of commandments and ordinances" (Ephesians 2:14-15).

We know that the word "law" had a variety of meanings in the Apostle Paul's day. Some of the explanation for these apparent contradictions is to be found there. But the real answer to Paul's seeming opposition to the Law is to be found in his innermost desire and concern: He was concerned that Christ, who had redeemed us, ever remain the focal point of our faith. Therefore he opposed the Judaizers, for they wanted to make the Law, in its widest sense, with its many special ordinances and provisions, the central point of the faith, and necessary for salvation. The Law, however, cannot redeem us. It cannot work righteousness in us. That can only happen through faith in Jesus Christ and His redemption.

So Paul takes pains to bring us to a new attitude toward the Law, by regarding it from the point of view of Calvary. The claims of righteousness and reward for keeping the Law must go. God is not gracious toward me because I keep this or that commandment. That would put it on the basis of "wages." But a relationship with God in His holiness can only be on the basis of grace. God is gracious toward me, despite my transgression of the commandments, because He forgives my sin on the basis of Jesus' sacrifice. Therefore everything depends upon my relationship to Jesus. And this is precisely true in regard to the Law, God's commandments. God's full judgment of my transgressions of the commandments was meted out to Jesus on the cross. He was there as my Substitute. Now everything depends upon this: Will I personally believe and accept this? I need His mercy and grace, for nothing good dwells in me (Romans 3:12). And through faith in what He now offers me, I become His, and His Spirit works in me the fruit of the new life. Now I fulfill the commandments through faith in Jesus' redemption, *and I do not rest from it*. This is the right attitude toward the Law. I fulfill the commandments out of love and thanks to Him. For they make known to me the will and wish of Him "who first loved me." "He who has my commandments and keeps them, he it is who loves me" (John 14:21). This was Paul's fundamental concern in regard to our attitude toward the Law.

Apart from this, he also opposed the Law insofar as the so-called "traditions and ordinances of the fathers" had actually become the traditions of men. This had degenerated into a scrupulous practice of the minutiae of individual regulations, void of power or joy. One had exchanged the letter for the spirit. But God also spoke out in the Old Testament against "The commandments of men learned by rote," and "the wisdom of their wise men" (Isaiah 29:13, 14). And Jesus said the same thing: "In vain do they worship me, teaching as doctrines the precepts of men" (Mark 7:7). As men add their traditions to God's commandments, the commandments can be misunderstood, misrepresented, even misused. But that is no ground for withdrawing with flimsy excuses from one's genuine obligation to the commandments.

Yet today the obligatory nature of the commandments is being questioned. This is happening to an extent within the Church itself. Some are seeking to make room in the Church for an unbiblical resistance to God's commandments. The root of this kind of thing goes deeper. It is not simply dissatisfaction with the accretion of "human traditions." It has to do with the nature of discipleship. To keep the commandments, to follow the will of Jesus, means to give up our rights. It means to set aside any standards or opinions of our own as to what is right and what we are to do. It means to give oneself over completely to His will, His wishes, His desires.

This is precisely what we do not want to do. This means death to our ego and our pride. And so, in league with our old Adam, we rebel against the commandments. Nothing so evokes rebellion from our hearts as a commandment which is laid upon us as an obligation. Besides that, today we are all more or less infected by the spirit of our times. For in Christian circles also, as we have seen, it is often man rather than God who is in the center. To a great extent we have allowed the wishes and standards and commandments of man to stand as valid. It has gone so far that "Sinai has lost its terror,"[1] and "Jesus has lost His authority as a great moral teacher."

When man occupies the central position, the drive of the impure ego is unmanageable. Human resolve and human

---

[1] Robinson, op. cit., p. 109

power avail nothing. God must occupy the central position — God in His holy love, God in judgment and mercy.

Now the commandments are a death knell to the Old Adam. Today it is heralded as a sign of "courage" to set aside the moral teachings of Jesus. But is it not rather a sign of cowardice? Is it not evidence that one is unprepared to face up to the challenge of Jesus' words? Jesus says, "Enter by the narrow gate. . . . Whoever does not give up all. . . . He who leaves all. . . ." When a man sidesteps such words, it indicates that he is not ready to let the Old Man die.

One cannot strike out Jesus' words about obedience, about the death of our will and desire. Jesus recognizes no discipleship which does not "take up the cross." This means to deny self. For Jesus draws a disciple into His own life. And what was that life? He denied self. He became poor. He was despised and abused. Yet He humbled Himself and was obedient. This is the meaning of discipleship — to give oneself to obedience, humiliation, self-denial, death.

But unlike ourselves, Jesus does not put a full stop here. We have not grasped the essential nature and the motive of His command to love. We hear only the call to take up the cross, deny self, and "fall into the ground and die" (John 12:24). We shrink from this. Then we are ready candidates for some "new teaching" regarding God's commandments: The commandments, after all, are an outmoded legalism; one cannot expect "modern man" to go along with them. But God's commandments are pure gospel. Their keynote is joy. For Jesus gives the clear command, "Enter at the narrow gate": But He goes on to point out that this gate leads to eternal life with God, full of purpose and joy.

By way of interpretation we can say: Enter at the narrow gate. Tread willingly the pathway which is narrow and difficult, which gives you no freedom to live out your impure wishes and desires. Along this narrow way you will find the fulfillment which your heart yearns for. For here you will find Jesus, who Himself is life and fulfillment. With Jesus, the Risen One, death is never the last word. He always leads through death to new, abundant life. A command of Jesus, at first glance, seems to be an aggravating prohibition. But when we live it out, we discover that it is in reality a signpost, directing us to a joy we never knew before.

One sees clearly in Jesus' word concerning one who leaves houses or brothers or sisters or father or mother or children or lands for His name's sake. For He goes on to say that such a one will "receive a hundredfold, and inherit eternal life" (Matthew 19:29). The same basic principle is seen in the word, "The meek — those who give up their 'rights' — shall inherit the earth" (Matthew 5:5). When one gives up his "rights," God Himself takes up the battle for those rights. How could it be otherwise? Jesus, the King of His Realm, is a King of love. It is only natural for His love and generosity to overflow to His subjects.

One sees it again in the word, "Give and it will be given to you" (Luke 6:38). Jesus says, "Give up . . . Do not seek earthly, transitory things; do not be concerned with them." At first one sees here renunciation, separation from earthly things, death. But immediately Jesus gives the assurance that the Father in heaven will take care of us, if we seek first the Kingdom of God and His righteousness. "All these things will be added unto you" (Matthew 6:25-33).

Jesus enunciated a great spiritual law when He said, "Unless a grain of wheat falls into the earth and dies, it remains alone. . . ." But the statement of the law does not end there. For He continues, "but if it dies, it bears much fruit" (John 12:24). Thus also, those who bore witness to Jesus' life on earth did not end their testimony with the report of His crucifixion and death, but only after they had proclaimed His resurrection. Yet for Jesus there was no resurrection, no fruit, no real life, and no joy except through death.

All the commandments issue forth from the Lord, who is the King of love. He rejoices to do good to the citizens of His realm (Jeremiah 32:41). That is the motive behind the commandments, which He sets out as guideposts for us. Jesus knows the human heart, self-centered and self-willed as it is. Yet He had the courage then, and also today in the twentieth century, to speak the truth to men: First there must be this death. The person wrapped up in self-love and self-concern is unhappy. We can only be happy in His Kingdom when we surrender our self-love up to death. Our self-love, for instance, wants to strike out whenever it suffers injustice. It will stand unmoveable upon its "rights," bitter and unforgiving, persisting in strife and hate. Indeed, our heart is full of evil. It is entangled in sin. It is under the power of Satan. In every situation it seeks to live out its desires and evil tendencies to the full. And the result is always the same: inner death.

In our day man is striving to "live life to the full." All desires must be developed, expressed, and lived to the full — desires of soul, body and mind. But Jesus is looking for men who will have the courage to lose, give up, sacrifice. He knows that something must die in us sinful men if we are to attain a new, joyful life. He seeks men who believe that His Word and His promise are Yea and Amen, who believe that He gives abundantly to those who in love yield everything to Him. He who loses his life — in things of soul, mind, and body — he it is who wins. His life will be rich and full of meaning.

O! let us believe the love of Jesus! He never demands or asks of us, but what He gives back many times over. "He always gives more than He takes." If we would just once try this venture of faith, we would discover that it works. After long years of hesitation, I experienced in my life that whoever dares to do what Jesus requires in His commandments will experience the fullness of His promises. I took the word, "Seek first the Kingdom of God." I sought to take it not as an ideal, but as an obligation. I began to orient my life accordingly. And I experienced its fulfillment. Everything needful was "added unto me," in ways I could not have imagined before. It happened in miraculous and unusual ways, according to the plans and fatherly care of God.*

In His Word the Lord says that we are not to revile when we are reviled, but trust to Him who judges justly (I Peter 2:21-23). My experience was similar in relation to this command. I learned again how God stands behind the Word which He gives as a command. I could say with the Psalmist: "Thou hast maintained my just cause; thou hast sat on the throne giving righteous judgment" (Psalm 9:4). As I suffered various injustices, and false reports and slander were circulated by certain persons, I remained silent and prayed for true love of my enemies so I could bless them. Then I saw how God defended me. The truth came to light. Some of my foes became my friends. My regret is that I did not go deeper into this venture of faith, for Jesus' promises are altogether trustworthy. Indeed, the sluices of heaven open, and a stream of blessing pours forth upon those who keep His commandments. The gates to the Kingdom of God open for them, both here and above (Revelation 22:14). The world today is a desert and a wasteland. One sees it in many aspects of man's common life. But for those who heed God's commandments, something of the Kingdom — a touch of Paradise — breaks forth right in the midst of the world.

True it is that the ways of faith, which lead to such joy, are often along dark pathways. We are repeatedly put to shame by His commandments. But thereby we learn what we are really like: sinful and bound to our old nature. From this knowledge, however, we gain a deeper and deeper contact with Jesus and the power of His redemption, which

---

*See *Realities: The Miracles of God Experienced Today*, by M. Basilea Schlink, Zondervan Publishing House, 1966.

makes us new creatures. Then His love finds room in us, so that we can give ourselves to Him, with all that we have. And thus are we made ready to do priestly service for Him.

"Workers Together With God" — Today's Greatest Need

TODAY JESUS NEEDS DISCIPLES who will do priestly service for Him. In the twilight of our times, man is looking for a way out. He looks to the wastelands of his own soul, and more and more he encounters a haunting silence. Only those who stand as priests before God still have power to snatch men out of the quicksands of despair. True disciples of Jesus seem to be the least "modern": The moral teachings of Jesus, and His commandments, are still holy and obligatory to them. Yet they are the only ones who can help modern man in his deep need. They can come to one virtually engulfed in the filth of sin, who is now seized with a nausea for it all. With full power they can speak the word of guilt and forgiveness which will set a man free. For they come from Jesus Christ, the Lamb of God, who has borne away all sin.

But woe unto him who bears the name of Christ and yet conforms to the spirit of the times. The prince of this world will befuddle him. He will fall under the power of the spirit of the world, which is directed by Satan. The end result will be that as a Christian in this world he will be powerless — salt without taste, no longer good for anything except to be thrown out and trodden under foot by men (Matthew 5: 13). "Living life to the full," in disregard of the commandments, makes one weak and unfit for anything. This applies particularly in Christianity. The power of "salt" grows only out of death, because the claim of God's commandments has been heeded. This alone equips us to do our service, and in this time of moral decay yet be for men a bridge to God and His Kingdom. It depends upon people who keep His commandments, in fully giving themselves and thereby sacrificing for others.

This kind of priestly attitude is the nature of people who make up the Kingdom of God. It is, indeed, a kingdom of priests (Exodus 19:6; I Peter 2:9; Revelation 1:6 and 5:10). Thus we meet priestly figures everywhere, both in the Old and New Testaments. Above all, our Lord Jesus Christ is set before us as the great High Priest. He suffered for the sins of mankind. As the heart of God grieved when He looked upon earth before the Flood, and saw mankind so corrupted by sin, so Jesus' life on earth was a suffering because of our sins. Therefore He sacrificed Himself out of love for His brethren. He could not suffer them to be destroyed by sin and guilt. And at the throne of God He continues to plead for His human children, because of His love for them (Romans 8:34; Hebrews 7:25).

Sin destroys God's creation. God hates sin so much, that because of it He gave His only begotten Son up to death. Sin therefore stimulates God's priestly people to a zeal and struggle against sin — out of love to a holy God, but also out of love to mankind who is heading for destruction. A priestly love is a rescuing love. It drives the priests of God to the zeal and sacrifice of their Master. We know how filled with grief Jesus was over the sins of His people. Their sins kindled a zeal in Him by which He drove the merchants and moneychangers out of the temple. A few hours before He had wept over His city.

This priestly people portray to the world the Kingdom of God. A great nobility rests upon them, a kingly splendor. For every priest is also a king. They are called His "kings and priests" (Revelation 1:6). They are to be like their Lord, who is both King and Priest.

Moses was such a figure — priest and king. As he came down from Sinai, "his anger burned hot, and he threw the tables out of his hands and broke them at the foot of the mountain. And he took the calf which they had made, and burnt it with fire, and ground it to power, scattered it upon the water, and made the people of Israel drink it" (Exodus 32:19-20). He was gripped by a burning anger against sin as his eyes fell upon the people dancing around the idol which they had fashioned after their own desires.

Phinehas presents another example of one who has a "priestly hate" for sin (Numbers 25). In Verse 1 we read: "While Israel dwelt in Shittim the people began to play the harlot with the daughters of Moab." They did this even though God's command strictly forbade them to do so. When it happened again, and a man brought a Moabite woman into the camp, Phinehas broke out in holy anger. As a true priest of God, he executed punishment, and killed both of them, as God had commanded. And the Lord said in regard to this: "Phinehas . . . has turned back my wrath from the people of Israel, in that he was jealous with my jealousy among them, so that I did not consume the people of Israel in my jealousy" (Verse 11). Phinehas knew that sin was an insult to the holy, living God. In sinning we make a covenant with Satan himself. But sin does not let just one soul topple into the destruction of hell: it drags others with it. One person who willingly gives way to sin becomes a bad leaven for a whole people. Where sin is discovered among God's people, which is not confessed and repented of, it must be rooted out.

The Apostle Paul wrote to the Church of Corinth in the same spirit, when a case of immorality came up: "And you are arrogant! Ought you not rather to mourn? Let him who has done this be removed from among you . . . you are not to associate with any one who bears the name of brother if he is guilty of immorality or greed, or is an idolater, reviler, drunkard, or robber — not even to eat with such a one. Drive out the wicked person from among you" (I Corinthians 5:2, 11, 13).

This is the attitude and conduct of priestly men, who represent the Kingdom of God. They react to sin in a way that is contrary to that of many Christians today. Today sin is frequently glossed over. Under the slogans of "concern for one's fellow man" and a falsely conceived "Christian compassion" sin is viewed as relatively harmless. In a false way — false because it does not comprehend the seriousness of the situation — one "pities" people who have sold themselves to sin. One excuses their sin on the basis of "psychological understanding," and renders it harmless on the basis of a "comprehensive grasp of man's existence."

But God is on the lookout for "fellow workers" (I Corinthians 3:9). God needs people who will really work with Him against sin. Sin is God's greatest sorrow. God seeks people who are gripped with the pain of their own sin and guilt, and that of their fellow man. He needs people who have a zeal to love and save, full of ardor in pleading and sacrifice, as members of the body of Christ, with Jesus Himself as Head and High Priest. God seeks priestly people, who will take an open stand against sin for the simple reason that they love God, and therefore they cannot bear that that God should be offended by the sin of a man.

Where are the believers today who are zealous for God's honor? Moses was concerned for God's honor: Therefore his anger was kindled when he saw the people dancing around the golden calf. Where are the believers who truly love their fellow men, and therefore cannot bear to see them ruined by the poison of sin — not only now, but also for all eternity? The Bible says that sin destroys body, soul and spirit, and makes us guilty over against others. But today this simple and basic truth is largely ignored. In actuality we do not reckon with the fact that sin will one day suffer a terrible judgment, and that, according to Jesus' word, a life of torment awaits sinners after their death.

We lack a priestly zeal against sin because in our hearts we lack compassion and tears for our fellow men. The same Moses who came down from the mountain and broke the tablets in fierce anger, could also intercede for his people and plead for mercy with self-sacrificing love (Exodus 32:32). This zeal is not to be confused with the zeal of professional zealots (Luke 9:54ff) such as one often finds in the sects. It is a priestly zeal, which is born alone from love.

To such a love and such a zeal God calls — today more than ever before. Our priestly calling, sealed with the blood of Jesus, must be taken up in earnest. God expects us to render this priestly service of self-sacrifice for others. It is a blessed service, by which I can become a "fellow worker" with God. With Him and in Him I can do this service. With Him I suffer wounds, in Him I lose my life, my rights, my claims, and my honor for my brother. "When reviled, we bless; when persecuted, we endure; when slandered, we try to conciliate; we have become, and are now, as the refuse of the world, the offscouring of all things" (I Corinthians 4:12-13). Yet "I endure everything for the sake of the elect, that they also may obtain salvation which in Christ Jesus goes with eternal glory" (II Timothy 2:10). This is the priestly service of the Apostle Paul. It takes courage, real courage. For men who accept the call to priestly service are prepared to give their lives in order that others might be saved.

In our day, Jesus waits for those who will dedicate themselves to such priestly service. Today sin, in all its degeneration and decadence, has attained proportions roughly equivalent to that which existed before the great Flood. Only priestly men can save mankind. If we pass by our nation, indeed if we pass by the whole of mankind and are not gripped by a grief for them, are not filled with a holy anger and zeal because of the extent of moral decadence, we will be guilty. Mankind is hurtling toward destruction of abysmal proportions. Sins that would make Sodom blush are glossed over and deemed relatively harmless. Who can justify such neglect in our day, to say nothing of before God's judgment throne? Such a one bears part of the guilt, and abets the uninhibited expansion of sin to unimaginable proportions.

Today, as sin shrieks to heaven, the true disciples of Jesus, as a priestly people, must cry out to God with tears and fasting. They must bow under their own sin as they intercede because of the sins of others. This is what Daniel did in his prayer of repentance (Daniel 9). If we do not do this, we are like the Priest and the Levite: They came upon the man who had fallen among robbers, who lay there in his blood, and passed by indifferently. Only today it is not one man lying there. Today our nation, indeed most all of mankind, lies in the "blood" of its sin and is almost drowning. The underlings in the realm opposing Jesus Christ do not lack zeal. Therefore ours must be an even more consuming zeal. "God seeks a man among us who can stand in the breach before Him for the land, that He should not destroy it" (Ezekiel 22:30). Where this priestly zeal is foreign to us, we must by all means pray for it. True compassion means pain and suffering — with God in His sorrow, with men who face destruction. This must fill us all. Ask and you shall receive!

The city of Jerusalem once faced destruction because of her sins. God commanded a man clad in linen, likely an angel: "Go through the city, through Jerusalem, and put a mark upon the foreheads of the men who sigh and groan over all the abominations that are committed in it" (Ezekiel 9:4). God is searching for such priestly people, who sigh and groan over all the abominations and sin in their city and country. Sin calls forth the judgment of God. Only a priestly people, who cry and sigh because of the sin, can stay the judgment. We should not pray for anything less than these men in Jerusalem received: Sorrow for my sins and the sins of my people, together with ardent supplication that the judgment be stayed. Such prayer has power to save still some people out of the sump of iniquity. It also means personal protection in times of great judgment, as we see in the case of the men in Jerusalem.

Moses had a zeal for his people, underscored with tears and supplication. But before he came to this, he had to climb up Mt. Sinai, shrouded in cloud and smoke, and meet God. Only thus could he intercede for his people as priest. In other words, he had to first go through the fires of judgment. He had to be cleansed by God's holiness for the great task which was to be given him. Afterward the deepest nature of God, which is love, was revealed to him. God revealed Himself to Moses in a way He had not to Abraham: "The Lord, the Lord, a God merciful and gracious, slow to anger, and abounding in steadfast love and faithfulness" (Exodus 34:6).

The way is thus clearly marked by which we receive God's love, by which we come to know His heart of love, and ourselves come to share this priestly love. It is the way of fire, which judges and purifies. A priestly man must come through the fire of God's holiness. Only thus can he break through to God's heart of love, and from there live out a life of priestly love. The priestly man must first of all face the holiness of God. This means that he must suffer his own life to come repeatedly under judgment. Only thus can he receive grace for the priestly work of prayer, tears and sacrifice. The fiery baptism of judgment is the way to become a priestly man. This is what Jesus proclaimed when He said: "Repent, the Kingdom of Heaven is at hand!"

The judgment of God is often executed where we least expect it. One can experience it, for instance, through the apparently unjust — or at least overdone — criticism of another person. It will come to us when the ugliness of our character is convincingly blazoned before ourselves and before men. Or we experience it in humiliations which God allows to come to us through people and situations, cutting across our well-meant intentions and goals. Only those who have themselves gone through this baptism of fire can lead others along this way into God's Kingdom. When priestly people themselves live in daily repentance, they will have the power to call others to turn from a life of sin.

The call which testifies to God's Kingdom, which summons men into the Kingdom, is always a call to repentance (Matthew 3:2; Acts 3:19-20). It is so in our day. We face a mature nihilism and a godlessness which more and more takes the upper hand. Everything hangs on this one call: Repent! Turn back from every way which is contrary to God's commandments! Come under the Lordship of Jesus Christ in His Kingdom, which rests on the foundation of God's commandments. Make haste! There is but little time! Judgment is at the door! It is the final hour!

III.

REALLY THE END OF TIME?
NOBODY BELIEVES IT

JESUS CHARACTERIZED the last days as a time when "iniquity shall abound" (Matthew 24:12). We have seen how this is true of our age, which is dominated to a frightening extent by immorality and crime. A general spirit of lawlessness already prevails in our time. We are approaching the state of affairs which the Bible says will be characteristic of the end times. This means that the judgment of God's wrath, proclaimed in the Revelation of John, is at the door. Destruction and doom impend. The time of the Antichrist is upon us. In that time, according to the Bible, the "great dragon" will persecute all those "who keep the commandments of God and bear testimony to Jesus" (Revelation 12:17). Those who keep God's commandments will be recognized by Satan as belonging to his great enemy, Jesus the Christ. Therefore he hates them. Thus a fateful decision hangs on our attitude toward the commandments. Do we truly belong to Christ and His Kingdom, or in the end will we be counted in the Antichrist's kingdom?

Jesus admonished us to pay attention to the signs of the end times. We live in an hour when His words carry an urgency they have never had before, because of the threat of an atomic war. Men of mature judgment, in the most diverse fields of thought and activity, speak of this decisive event. Reinhold Schneider spent a lifetime seeking knowledge of the hidden workings of spiritual power. Before his death he said,

"I am convinced that the end of history is near. Our time is the interval between the end of the realm and the last jerk of the clock-hand."[1] Men like Kierkegaard, Burkhardt, Thomas Mann, and R. M. Rilke convey a somber mood of death. They were all gripped by the intuition that "not only was a century coming to its end, but with it a world was sinking, the very constitution of the world was being altered."[2] Alexander Ruestov said that it was an "empirically established fact" that our situation is " 'eschatological' in the fullest apocalyptic sense of that word."[3]

This is simply the fact of our time. Today one can hardly get away from the reality that "The existence of the atomic bomb represents an immediate danger to all people. The situation is here. It cannot be reversed. Man is able to wipe mankind and all life from the face of the globe by his own action. The bare circumstances indicate that this end will come within the next decade."[4] True, men can be mistaken. Men are limited in knowledge and understanding. It might be unimportant that men of our time speak of a great darkness which is rapidly approaching.

But another prophesied a time of terror and darkness for mankind, namely God Himself, the Lord and Creator. He, above all, has said it — the Lord who cannot be mistaken. His nature is in no way limited. What He has established cannot be changed. It is God who alone is all-knowing and all-mighty, who brings us these predictions and prophecies. His word remains valid for time and eternity.

No one else has made prophecies thousands of years beforehand, which have been confirmed by the course of history. Only the Lord God could speak with such majesty:

---

[1] Baehr *Wo stehen wir heute?*, op. cit., p. 70
[2] Baehr, op. cit., p. 160-61
[3] Baehr, op. cit., p. 70
[4] Baehr, op. cit., Karl Jaspers p. 41

"I am the first and I am the last; besides me there is no god. Who is like me? Let him proclaim it, let him declare it and set it forth before me. Who has announced from of old the things to come? Let them tell us what is yet to be. Fear not, nor be afraid; have I not told you from of old and declared it? And you are my witnesses!" (Isaiah 44:6-8).

In our times we are witnesses that God's prophecies for Israel have been fulfilled. In Deuteronomy 28:64-65, God said, "And the Lord will scatter you among all peoples, from one end of the earth to the other . . . and among these nations you shall find no ease." And likewise in verse 37 He says, "And you shall become a horror, a proverb, and a byword among all the peoples where the Lord will lead you away." We read further in Leviticus 26:31-32, "I will lay your cities waste, and I will make your sanctuaries desolate. . . . And I will devastate the land, so that your enemies who settle in it shall be astonished at it."

That is precisely what came to pass in the course of history. The land of Israel was laid waste. Her cities were turned to rubble. And her people were dispersed into virtually every nation of the world. One sees this clearly in the new State of Israel: Jews from more than seventy nations have returned to the land of their fathers. For thousands of years they have been enslaved, despised, persecuted.

The prophecies concerning Israel were truly fulfilled. The prophecies concerning us and all nations will also be fulfilled. For the Lord did not prophesy alone concerning Israel. He also prophesied concerning the whole world in these latter days. In these prophecies He speaks of a time in which the nations would become unified. In these prophecies He speaks concerning the entire inhabited earth. He says, "The clamor will resound to the ends of the earth, for the Lord has an indictment against the nations; he is entering into judgment with all flesh, and the wicked he will put to the sword. Behold, evil is going forth from nation to nation, and a great tempest is stirring from the farthest parts of the earth" (Jeremiah 25:31-32).

"Put in the sickle, for the harvest is ripe. Go in, tread, for the winepress is full. The vats overflow, for their wickedness is great" (Joel 3:13). "Behold, the day of the Lord comes, cruel, with wrath and fierce anger, to make the earth a desolation and to destroy its sinners from it . . . I will punish the world for its evil, and the wicked for their iniquity; I will put an end to the pride of the arrogant, and lay low the haughtiness of the ruthless . . . and the earth will be shaken out of its place, at the wrath of the Lord of hosts in the day of his fierce anger" (Isaiah 13:9, 11, 13).

In the New Testament, Jesus says exactly the same thing concerning the end times. He also says that fear and destruction will be visited upon the entire inhabited earth (Luke 21:26). This is our situation today. Mankind has become a family of nations in our time. And the whole family is saturated with one spirit, the spirit of immorality and lawlessness. The end times, according to Jesus, will be like the times of Noah (Luke 17:26-27). The characteristic of that age was that "the earth was corrupt" (Genesis 6:12). The word in our day is "decadence," which means corruption.

Our times also have a common fear and worry. Today a fearful atomic war hangs like a sword of Damocles over all the nations of the earth. These are facts which cannot be ignored.

Jesus says, "When you see all these things, you know that he (Jesus) is near, at the very gates" (Matthew 24:33). Thus it is the Lord who wants to rouse and alert us with all the facts. He calls us in this hour: The end times are here! Stay awake! Be ready! The whole of God's plan is about to be fulfilled!

God is our Father. He does not want to destroy, but to save. Yet He knows how "hard of hearing" we are. He knows that we do not want to hear the truth about mankind, and about the hour in which we live. That is why He took such pains to establish the truth in prophecy. Thousands of years beforehand, He detailed the individual happenings which would prepare the way for the final judgment. It is unfathomable how God predicted the events of our atomic and space age thousands of years beforehand. His words demand our attention today, whatever our individual interpretation of the apocalyptic passages in the Bible might be. In any case, the apocalyptic passages have greater impact on us today than they did thirty years ago. Today it is not purely an intervention of God which could bring about the fulfillment of these passages — something which goes beyond our human comprehension. The stockpiles of atomic weapons all over the world have created a perfectly natural situation which could unleash such apocalyptic events.

In His love and mercy, God has done everything possible to warn people to be prepared. In this regard, the well-known atomic physicist, Bernhard Philberth said: "Today, in the decade after 1960, physics and technology are running in astonishing and unexpected parallel with the Parousia-proclamations of Christ, and the veiled sayings of the Book of Revelation. . . . Christian prophecy may have seemed fantastic symbolism in former times, and even until quite recently. It yielded no clear meaning. Yet today, in a madly rushing technological age, it is a factual report which can stand any sober comparison."[5]

In the time of Jesus, and even more in the time of the Old Testament prophecies 500-600 years earlier, the origin and effects of such events were completely beyond man's understanding. One knew nothing of nuclear energy, with its power in a single bomb to wipe out great cities, indeed the population of the entire inhabited earth. One knew nothing

---

[5]Philberth, *Christliche Prophetie und Nuklearenergie*, Christiana Verlag-Zuerich 1963, p. 9 and 26

of a deadly atomic dust which could turn fields and meadows into a wilderness. One knew nothing of space ships which could journey to the moon. One knew nothing of the possibility that other planets could come under our influence, and be made to suffer with us at the hands of atomic weapons.

No one would have believed that one day there would be weapons which would put man in the position of being able to destroy virtually the entire inhabited earth with the push of a button. No one would have been believed who contended that man could darken the sun, or that moon and stars could come within our grip. And yet all of this was prophesied thousands of years ago.

Thus it was, that up until ten or twenty years ago most of the prophecies in the Revelation of John were interpreted almost exclusively in a symbolic sense. Today, however, these prophecies describe real possibilities which could take place in our own time. What a fearsome threat these words carry, when we realize that their meaning is not symbolic, but an acute reality which lies fully within the sphere of present-day technology:

"The sun and the moon are darkened, and the stars withdraw their shining" (Joel 2:10).

"The sun shall be turned to darkness" (Joel 2:31). Today it is quite possible that sun, moon and stars could be obscured by masses of radioactive dust resulting from the explosion of hydrogen bombs.

"All the host of heaven shall rot away, and the skies roll up like a scroll" (Isaiah 34:4). In our day intercontinental ballistic missiles and satellites have penetrated into the realm of the stars at fantastic speeds.

"And I will give portents in the heavens and on the earth, blood and fire and columns of smoke" (Joel 2:30). Today the flash of light from an atomic explosion is thirty times as brilliant as the sun — and becomes a rising atomic mushroom of fire and smoke.

"For by fire will the Lord execute judgment" (Isaiah 66:16). The fireball of a hydrogen bomb explosion, at 100 million degrees centigrade, produces enough heat to consume anything.

"Behold, the Lord will lay waste the earth and make it desolate, and he will twist its surface and scatter its inhabitants" (Isaiah 24:1). One hundred thousand atomic bombs, and many thousands of hydrogen bombs, are at the ready — more than enough to make the earth uninhabitable.

"The earth shall be utterly laid waste and utterly despoiled" (Isaiah 24:3). A leading politician has said that the first atomic attack would leave 700 to 800 million dead in its wake. The fearsome specter for millions is that atomic rockets can flash across continents and oceans in minutes, turning whole countries into craters of death. Survivors will live in hiding places, amidst a world of ruin and death.

"And those slain by the Lord on that day shall extend from one end of the earth to the other. They shall not be lamented or gathered or buried; they shall be dung on the surface of the ground" (Jeremiah 25:33).

"The Lord is enraged against all their host, he has doomed them, has given them over for slaughter. Their slain shall be cast out, and the stench of their corpses shall rise; the mountains shall flow with their blood" (Isaiah 34:2-3). Physicists such as Dr. Oppenheimer have raised the question whether there will be enough survivors to bury the millions of dead after an atomic war.

"I will lay waste mountains and hills, and dry up all their herbage" (Isaiah 42:15). Today clouds of radioactive dust orbit the earth. They threaten to descend after a period of years as a deadly precipitation, destroying all vegetation.

The reality of things which God prophesied 2500 years ago is close at hand. The same is true of prophecies which Jesus Christ spoke in the gospels and through His apostles nearly 2000 years ago. Jesus said: "The sun will be darkened and the moon will not give its light, and the stars will fall from the heaven" (Matthew 24:29, Mark 13:25). In Revelation 8:12 we read, "The fourth angel blew his trumpet, and a third of the sun was struck, and a third of the moon, and a third of the stars, so that a third of their light was darkened." The Apostle Peter writes, "The elements will be dissolved with fire, and the earth and the works that are upon it will be burned up" (II Peter 3:10, 12). "The second angel blew his trumpet, and something like a great mountain, burning with fire, was thrown into the sea" (Revelation 8:8). This prophecy of the Apostle John, according to atomic physicist Philberth, is an apt description of a hydrogen bomb explosion.[6]

Jesus' words describe the effect upon people of such explosions in space: ". . . but on the day when Lot went out from Sodom fire and brimstone rained from heaven and destroyed them all — so will it be on the day when the Son of man is revealed" (Luke 17:29-30). The Book of Revelation completes the picture: ". . . a third of the earth was burnt up, and a third of the trees were burnt up, and all green grass was burnt up" (Revelation 8:7). This corresponds to the estimates of atomic physicists regarding the use of atomic weapons. When the "bowls of wrath" are poured out in the Book of Revelation, the earth is completely destroyed, so that even the rivers dry up, and "every island fled away, and no mountains were to be found" (Revelation 16:12, 20).

Considering all these words, and the prophecies which have been fulfilled in regard to Israel, it becomes evident that God's warning is meant for us. "Remember the former things of old; for I am God, and there is none like me, declaring the end from the beginning and from ancient times things not yet done, saying, 'My counsel shall stand, and I will accomplish all my purpose' " (Isaiah 46:9-10).

---
[6]Philberth, op. cit., p. 172

"Behold, the former things have come to pass, and new things I now declare; before they spring forth I tell you of them" (Isaiah 42:9). Indeed God's prophecies have come to pass. This is plain to see in the history of Israel right in our own time. During the dreadful murder of millions of Jews throughout Europe, who would have thought that instead of being exterminated they would return to the land of their fathers from all corners of the world? (Ezekiel 11:16-17). In like manner the yet unfulfilled prophecies regarding the nations will be fulfilled in the end times.

The mighty acts of God, in fulfilling His prophecies, bring us face to face with the great, eternal, almighty God. Since Nietzsche the mocking call has been heard — and now its strident voice is raised even by theologians and churchmen — "God is dead!" But God proves, "Behold, I live!" Today men mockingly say, "God is silent." In rebellion and hatred against God, they think they can do as they please. But God is not mocked.

What we can scarcely comprehend is the unfathomable humility and patience of God. It is born out of His love. Through the centuries He has borne this mockery and ridicule. And still He bears it in our godless age. Still He waits. . . before the terrible judgment descends.

Equally incomprehensible — in the face of this patience and concern which God directs toward us — is the blindness of man: In the long run we want to make God responsible for sin and depravity. We rebel against God, throw faith and the commandments of God overboard; we clear the way to live life the way we want to, to sin as we choose — which brings us nothing but destruction, emptiness and senselessness. And then, having made our bed, we blame God that we must lie in it; He is silent; He no longer speaks to anyone. But the hour is near when God will break silence. For the harvest is ripe. The sin and blasphemy of man cries out to heaven.

In February, 1964, an Israeli newspaper reviewed the American film, "How I Learned to Love the Bomb." They said, "It was the hand of the satyr, laid upon the holiest possessions of the nation." That hand will be brought low in the terror of an atomic war. Atomic weapons will not only bring a horrible death to millions, but will also slowly, torturously destroy the lives of those who survive.

God alone knows the hour. But the signs which He Himself has given indicate that it is near. In that hour He will prove Himself to be the living God. Then He will reveal that His silence was not due to weakness or incompetence, as scoffers have said since the Age of the Enlightenment. Then it will be revealed that He did not fail in His government of the world. For then He will show that He has guided the world according to a clearly defined plan — a plan marked by His wisdom, and above all by His great love. Then it will be recognized that His longsuffering and patience held back the judgment of atomic war upon the earth until "the bowl of evil was filled to overflowing" — just as He prophesied thousands of years beforehand.

Only then will He step in. Then this corrupt earth will be devastated with weapons of destruction which the fallen human creature — inspired by Satan — has himself created. That will be the end of man, though he was commissioned by God to subdue the earth and have dominion over it. But now Lucifer has led him to develop weapons which will destroy the earth. When mankind as a whole is drunk with power, the depraved human spirit, as a last act of insanity, will destroy the earth. That will be the end of the "autonomy" and "self-determination" of reason. That will be the end of Nietzsche's idea of the "superman."

This is the end of "living one's life to the full." This is where denial of the living, self-revealing God leads — a denial instigated by the seemingly harmless theories of rationalism and idealism. This is where a revolution in ethics, which reaches right into the heart of theology, leads — to this and nothing else. Yet no one wants to believe it — just as once before none would believe it. . . .

So it was in the city of Jerusalem in the year A.D. 63. The festival was in full swing. Pilgrims streamed into the city by the thousands for the festival. Crowds gathered in the streets and in the temple square. The festival spirit dominated the entire city.

But then a shrill cry echoed down the streets: "Woe! Woe unto this city! Woe unto those who dwell therein!" It was a peasant from the country. A lunatic? They brought him before the authorities. They ordered him flogged. He made no plea for himself. He shed no tears. But with every lash of the whip he cried out in a voice of lament, "Woe! Woe to the city!" The historians of antiquity, Josephus and Tacitus, report this event.

Why did this man cry out against the city? The city faced no danger. It enjoyed peace and prosperity. Or did it? A fearful prophecy of Jesus hung in glowing letters above this city: "For the days shall come upon you, when your enemies will cast up a bank about you and surround you, and hem you in on every side, and dash you to the ground, you and your children within you, and they will not leave one stone upon another in you" (Luke 19:43-44).

Just a word — nothing more? Sound and fury? Years had passed by since the words were uttered. Nothing had happened. Those who had heard of this prophecy of Jesus might well have mocked: "He prophesied destruction, the Nazarene, but we have never had it so good!"

There was something else remarkable about the incident. Josephus and Tacitus report it: A star which had the shape of a sword, and a comet, hung in the sky over the city for a whole year. But in that year nothing took place which altered the good fortune of the city.

But then a day came, a day that began like any other. It was the 14th of April, A.D. 70. Something happened. It was on a Friday, before the Feast of Passover. Strangely, it was on the same day that Jesus was crucified, He who had spoken the prophecy concerning Jerusalem. But who thought of it?

Suddenly the Roman army hove into sight. In three columns they advanced on the city. Again, strangely, one of the columns made camp at roughly the same spot on the Mount of Olives where Jesus had prophesied that a bank would be cast up around the city. Now the bank was there. The picture of the city changes. Terror and fear of hunger reign. Thousands of women and children are burnt alive on the roof of one of the Temple buildings. More than 500 crosses ring the city around, and on them hang the citizens of Jerusalem. The entire city and Temple are destroyed, leveled to the ground. On April 13th no one would have believed it.

Why did it happen? It happened because beforehand none would believe it and heed the call to repentance. Thus the horrible destruction of the city, with more than a million people come together for the Passover Feast, was fulfilled. Jesus had prophesied this destruction even to minor details, and proclaimed to the inhabitants of Jerusalem, "This will come to pass because you did not know the time of your visitation." Jesus had come with the call, "Repent! The Kingdom of God is at hand!" They would not believe that ignoring that call could bring such catastrophic results.

Following the prophecy concerning Jerusalem, Jesus prophesied just as clearly concerning later times. Jesus called the judgment of Jerusalem "days of vengeance. . . great distress shall be upon the earth, and wrath upon this people" (Luke 21:22, 23). Then Jesus told, as we have already seen, how the judgment of God's wrath will fall on all inhabitants of the earth in the end times.

"And they did not know —" (Matthew 24:39). This is the frightening part of Jesus' prophecy for the last times, when great destruction will fall. They do not know it today either, though thousands of missiles are poised for firing. It is as it was in Jesus' time: No one wants to believe it. Yet who can deny that terrible destruction threatens our cities and nations? If again today no one will believe it, then we too will be lost. Jesus' word will be fulfilled.

Therefore — O! let us *believe* Jesus' word! If we but knew the hour of our visitation, we would repent. It is repentance which alone saves from judgment. Repentance gives the power for priestly intercession, which alone can stay the judgment. Repentance gives entrance into His Kingdom, where peace and joy reign, where we remain safe in the Father's hand, even in the most difficult times. Repentance makes us citizens of the Kingdom which shall never end, which shall be visibly established when Jesus Christ comes again as King of kings and Lord of lords. "Blessed are those who keep His commandments and bear testimony to Jesus."

APPENDIX

INTRODUCTION TO THE ORIGINAL EDITION

IN THIS FIRST American edition of an English translation of one of her books, Mother Basilea Schlink has given us a book which is both courageous and helpful — courageous because it dares to present an unvarnished picture of civilized western life as it is lived today, and helpful because Mother Basilea is not content simply to paint dark portraits of the world but points the way for the Christian to live effectively, even victoriously, in the midst of that world.

The portrayal of contemporary life, as she marshals page after page of details and statistics regarding man's sin and rebellion against God, is almost unbelievable. Can it be that such is the human situation and that therefore the judgment of God hangs ominously above the seemingly triumphant tides of today's history? It is not strange that the title of the book proclaims *And None Would Believe It*. We may not agree with Mother Basilea's interpretations in all details, but the essential picture she presents is corroborated in a thousand books, magazines, newspapers, mass media and official records being filed away every day in our western world. Whether we believe it or not, if we accept the reality of the existence of God, man's sin stands forth in all its undeniable horror; and if moral principles do exist in a world like ours, how can judgment fail to be impending?

Mother Basilea does not attempt to prescribe a remedy for the world as a whole, but she does have a vital and effective solution to offer to the Christian, both the individual and the Christian community. The remedy in simple words is penitence — the acknowledgment and confession of our sins and the renewal of life that comes from this experience.

And this remedy is not a theoretical matter for Mother Basilea. She and her associates in the founding of the Ecumenical Sisterhood of Mary drew this lesson from the deep "wells of salvation" that opened to them as a result of their living through the bombing experience at Darmstadt in 1944. No doubt each of them has had to relearn the lesson — including Mother Basilea herself, according to her own confession. But it has proved to be for them a spring of life, of healing and renewal; and as a result, the home of the Sisterhood in Darmstadt has become an enriching blessing to the whole church in Germany and beyond.

Furthermore, the ministry of penitence and guilt-bearing which the Sisters have assumed in relation to the Jewish people in Israel has become a special source of renewal of brotherhood between Israel and the German people. It has opened doors too, for a unique hearing of the witness of the sisters among the people of Israel.

From time to time down through the Christian centuries the Holy Spirit reveals anew some great truth of the Gospel to some individual, some branch or group within the church. New fires are kindled as a result, new strength experienced, new visions seen. The reality of both the power and the fellowship of the Holy Spirit is felt and experienced anew and the whole church becomes indebted to those who are willing to walk more fully in the ways of God. Such a new manifestation of "renewal in the Holy Spirit" is being given to us today through the Ecumenical Sisterhood of Mary. Its fearless denunciation of the prevailing sins of the times, its challenge to a life of whole-hearted sacrifice, its vision for and understanding of the new ecumenical age, and its willingness in a time of materialism and self-indulgence to call men to an uncompromising walk with God, give a power and convincing quality to its witness which it is difficult to withstand.

The sisters of Darmstadt have a message from God for our time. Their stern proclamation of judgment blended with their earnest call to penitence reminds us of the words of Isaiah in "the Old Testament Apocalypse" (chapters 24 and 27). It is a mighty word of both terror and promise. Mother Basilea has brought that word already through a large number of books and publications. We are glad that it will now be published also here in America, where surely our churches can profit both by the life of devoted service to Christ which the Sisters so strongly exemplify, and by the prophetic denunciation of the evils of our time which Mother Basilea's pen so effectively proclaims.

BERNHARD CHRISTENSEN

Luther Theological Seminary
St. Paul, Minnesota

FOREWORD TO THE ORIGINAL EDITION

TODAY PEOPLE ARE SEEKING a light which can penetrate the darkness and confusion of our age. This book is intended for such honest seekers.

It deals with realities which affect our everyday life. It sees the world as a world which God loves, a world He suffers over, a world He would fain care for and protect.

Some who pick up this book may not grasp its purpose at once. Mother Basilea sounds a call for this hour of human history. It is rooted in her own clearly-defined faith. She evaluates the things of which she speaks from the standpoint of this faith. The frank manner in which she expresses her faith may be strange to some. But should this not rather be a cause for rejoicing? Doesn't our age cry out for just this: a well-considered word which takes its stand on the firm rock of faith?

What Mother Basilea writes here carries the burden of a prophetic message which she has received and now must pass on. The message is for this moment in human history. There is no possibility of being a casual observer of the events of our time. Decision — fateful decision — will be required of all of us. Ever and again through the centuries of the Church's history, God has quickened the word of prophecy. Through men, He has sounded a warning and given a word of wisdom which would guide men in the hour through which they must pass. Mother Basilea does not presume to set forth dogmatic and final statements, and certainly not concerning the Second Coming of Jesus. She lays out no pat scheme, saying, "Thus and so must everything come to pass." It is rather this: God has laid a burning message upon her heart and conscience. It is a message which must be delivered and passed on.

Some may have a different religious viewpoint than Mother Basilea. There will be differing positions with regard to the prophetic vision which she expresses. But these differences only highlight our common need — more urgent than ever before — to gain a clear insight into the real issues of our day. For we will all be called to final account for our decision, not only before men, but before God Himself.

Some may feel that Mother Basilea does not adapt her language and expression to the needs of "modern man." But it would be unnatural to affect a manner of expression which is not really one's own. Perhaps some could wish that Mother Basilea would state certain theological questions more precisely. But precisely that is contrary to her purpose. She knows that God has not called her to enter the theological discussions of our present day. Rather, her commission has been to call people to "hear and obey." This call would lead one to a clear-cut decision for God, and a renewed and deepened dedication to Him.

At the same time, Mother Basilea makes clear that Jesus answers the obedient hearer with clear proofs of His presence and reality. One can literally experience the ruling power of God, the Kingdom of Heaven — and this means true peace and joy in the midst of today's dark world. Thereby our lives focus upon the Coming Lord, and we begin to comprehend the true dimension of the future. For our existence as Christians and as a Body of Believers is inevitably and creatively bound to this "true future." And we move toward it in our day with an urgency.

With a view to this goal, Mother Basilea seeks to share a word from God. She presents an answer to the critical problems which hem us in on all sides in the world today. She points to a real way out.

MOTHER M. MARTYRIA

Other books you may want to read...

I'M NOT MAD AT GOD
by David Wilkerson
In this unique book David Wilkerson opens up his heart to tell us of the inner conflicts and victories. Its message has a keen cutting edge and a practicality not often found in books with a devotional flavor. Over 100,000 copies sold in hard cover. 75¢

AFTER ITS KIND
by Byron C. Nelson
A clear and thorough discussion of the theory of evolution. It is not merely critical, it is constructive. It meets and refutes the evolutionist on his own ground and gives the best authorities for every position taken. $1.95

THE DELUGE STORY IN STONE
by Byron C. Nelson
This book, along with AFTER ITS KIND, is a classic in the area of defending a creationist point of view and is usually quoted by contemporary writers on the subject. $1.95

STARS, SIGNS, AND SALVATION IN THE AGE OF AQUARIUS
by James Bjornstad and Shildes Johnson
Astrology—where did it all begin? Is astrology really valid? Is it compatible with Judaism and Christianity? Read and consider the authors' sometimes unsettling but always logical conclusions. 95¢

Purchase these books at YOUR LOCAL BOOKSTORE.

If your local bookstore does not have these books, you may order from
BETHANY FELLOWSHIP, INC.
6820 Auto Club Road
Minneapolis, Minnesota 55438

Enclose payment with your order plus 10¢ per book for postage.